Eyes on the Child

Three Portfolio Stories

Kathe Jervis

Foreword by Linda Darling-Hammond
Afterword by Joseph McDonald

Teachers College, Columbia University
New York and London

To Bob, Alexa, and Lisa

Published by Teachers College Press, 1234 Amsterdam Avenue, New York, NY 10027

Copyright © 1996 by Teachers College, Columbia University

Library of Congress Cataloging-in-Publication Data

Jervis, Kathe.
    Eyes on the child : three portfolio stories / Kathe Jervis : foreword by
Linda Darling-Hammond : afterword by Joseph McDonald.
      p.   cm. — (The series on school reform)
      Includes bibliographical references (p.   ) and index.
      ISBN 0-8077-3515-9 (cloth : alk. paper). — ISBN 0-8077-3514-0 (pbk. :
alk. paper)
      1. Portfolios in education—United States—Case studies. 2. Educational
tests and measurements—United States—Case studies. 3. Educational change—
United States—Case studies. I. Title. II. Series
    LB1029.P67J47   1996   96-3444
    371.2'62—dc20

ISBN 0-8077-3514-0 (paper)
ISBN 0-8077-3515-9 (cloth)

Printed on acid-free paper

Manufactured in the United States of America

03 02 01 00 99 98 97 96   8 7 6 5 4 3 2 1

the series on school reform

Patricia A. Wasley
Coalition of
Essential Schools

Ann Lieberman
NCREST

SERIES EDITORS

Joseph P. McDonald
Annenberg Institute
for School Reform

This series also incorporates earlier titles in the
Professional Development and Practice Series

Contents

Acknowledgments

The teachers portrayed here—Marla English, Barb Renfrow-Baker, Mildred Sanders, and Cathy Skowron—have been wonderful. Without their willingness and cooperation there would be no book.

For invaluable help in shaping the manuscript, I thank: Terry Baker, David Bensman, Pat Carini, Ted Chittenden, Linda Darling-Hammond, Lynn Einbender, Maxine Greene, Ann Lieberman, Joe McDonald, Diane Mullins, Char Myers, Linda Nathan, Kim Powell, Rob Southworth, Nancy Wilson, and Diane Wood read early drafts. Nancy Place helped me understand the nuances of portfolios in a continuation of our decades-long collegial talk.

Support for the Four Seasons Project came from the DeWitt Wallace-Reader's Digest Fund and the Metropolitan Life Foundation.

I would also like to thank my family, who are unacknowledged in my previous work though they have been giving me editorial help for years: my husband, Bob; my father-in-law, Herman; and my daughters, Alexa and Lisa (now old enough to be superb editors).

FOREWORD

On Assessment
and Accountability

In this book, Kathe Jervis chronicles teachers' efforts to develop new strategies for looking at children's work and learning in three schools across the country—schools that are involved in radical restructuring of education in concert with networks of reformers (the Coalition of Essential Schools, Foxfire, and Project Zero) with the support of an interlocking network of courageous teachers. In the course of the stories, she captures the dilemmas experienced by teachers working on the fault line between policy and practice at the time when a tectonic clash of paradigms is at work.

The assessment strategies these teachers are inventing are "authentic" in that they examine what students can do when they are engaged in real-world activities and the creation of their own ideas and products. Rather than having students take multiple-choice tests in which they react to the questions and answers of others, student work and thinking are examined as they develop research, do science, read and discuss, build things, write in a variety of forms, pose questions, and wrestle with mathematical ideas. Teachers inquire into this work to assess its meaning for learning as well as for teaching.

In many cases, the assessment strategies described here are so firmly embedded in the curriculum that they are practically indistinguishable from instruction. In this way, they provide students and teachers with a genuine rather than a contrived opportunity to see what kind of learning is occurring and what kind of performance is developing. They provide many sources of evidence and different kinds of indicators about what students know and can do, and they illuminate how students think as well as what they know. As teachers invent and refine these strategies, they are reshaping the purposes as well as the forms of assessment—bending it to the service of teaching and learning rather than to the goals of labeling, selecting, and sorting.

Their efforts are redefining accountability as well as assessment. Assessment as a lens for understanding students creates learner-centered accountability strategies that could ultimately replace the bureaucratic approaches that were developed nearly a century ago. Rather than looking up the hierarchy for direction about what and how to teach, these teachers are keeping their "eyes on the child" as the primary guide for their teaching decisions. The professional accountability they are developing—one that attends knowledgeably to what students need rather than to what procedures demand—poses an alternative to the system of hierarchically determined rules for practice managed through externally developed texts and tests. In the bureaucratic conception, teachers are accountable for following the procedures—curriculum guidelines, placement and promotion rules, evaluation methods—and students are to be processed by them. The standard for gauging practice is compliance rather than effectiveness.

Early on in the development of this system, curriculum and assessment decisions were removed from the hands of teachers and placed under the control of bureaucratic agencies and commercial companies. This allowed external authorities to determine what should be taught and learned, and provided "objective" means for classifying students. In contrast to teachers abroad, who have long developed and evaluated the rich array of performance assessments in which their students engage, U.S. teachers have been conduits for tests designed and scored by others for the primary purpose of placing students in programs, tracks, and grades.

From an era in which testing was the major tool for controlling curriculum and teaching work, sorting students, and rationing learning opportunities, these hardy warriors are moving into a brave new world in which assessment is a means for identifying student strengths and learning strategies, expanding curriculum possibilities, and informing more varied teaching. Rather than keeping teaching under control, these new assessments take teaching and learning "out of control" by expanding the horizons of both. They empower teachers with greater understanding of both their students and of learning generally. This makes the prescribed practices of bureaucratic systems unwarranted and implausible.

It is no wonder that the teachers in these stories find themselves on the horns of many dilemmas. They need to reconcile the current system with the new possibilities their work presents. They are dealing with the uncertainties that arise when simple, standardized methods are not the only ones for gauging quality and progress. They are confronting new issues of standard-setting, equity, and motivation in a world where rigidity and relativity trade off differently. They are seeking and finding new and different resolutions of the dialectic between systems' legitimate desires for common standards, on the one hand, and students' very real needs for contextually appropriate practice, on the other.

Concerns for equity tend to pull policymakers toward strategies that emphasize uniformity and standardization. Concerns for meeting the needs of unique students and for building learning from the experiences of diverse learners pull teachers toward strategies that emphasize variability and contextualization. Both are necessary concerns. As the new era changes the terms of the discourse, both policymakers and practitioners must find more educationally useful strategies for enacting their desires for standards and supports for students. New tightropes must be strung and walked.

These stories provide fertile ground for imagining how the brave new world might be begun. If we keep our eyes on the child, the dialectic will be a healthy one that continually challenges schools to find richer ways to develop standards without standardization, and to support students while stretching them to become all that they can be.

Linda Darling-Hammond

Prologue to the Stories

Teachers across the country are creating new knowledge in their own classrooms, but as the editors' introduction to the Spring, 1994 *Harvard Educational Review* special issue "Equity in Educational Assessment" makes clear, researchers' preoccupation with large-scale assessment policies leaves out any vital discussion of teachers' efforts, experiences, and insights. This collection of three case studies seeks to rectify that absence. The first half of each story locates the teachers within the context of their school and classroom in order to draw out some basic issues they face as they put portfolios into practice and attempt to satisfy others that they are responsive and responsible to the public that both finances schools and sends its children through their doors. The second half of each story describes the portfolios in each classroom that have grown out of particular circumstances, including the values that guide teachers and the dilemmas that vex them.

Teachers are not creating this new knowledge alone. On an unseasonably cold July morning at the University of Washington, 20 or so K–12 teachers, researchers, and university professors crowd into a small conference room. Sitting around a table, on the floor, or along the wall, they turn toward 8-year-old Sophia's 14" × 20" painting, propped up against the blackboard. Steve Seidel, a Project Zero researcher, prompts the group to describe Sophia's work without interpreting or speculating on it, but we cannot resist our own judgments. Is it Matisse-like (as I have in my notes) or Van Gogh-like as someone else suggests? Is it a castle? Toe prints in the sky? A red road? Rapunzel hiding? As the group begins to recognize the aim of this formal description, individuals increasingly note Sophia's arrangement of colors, shapes, and lines on the page. More neutral words—"blotches," "spots," and "spaces"—come into play.

Then Sophia's second-grade teacher, Cathy Skowron— an artist herself— explains how Sophia came to produce this response to a March night sky in Provincetown, Massachusetts.

> I looked with my class at the solar system in books, models, and films, and then we met one night after dark to observe the night sky. The next day, I introduced a book of Van Gogh's work, including *Starry*

Night, and noticed the children's interest in how Van Gogh's painting changed as he aged. I then showed a segment of a PBS video on artists and mental illness, which moved my (by then) teary-eyed students to ask about Van Gogh's life. Children began to think more about why Van Gogh painted the way he did. When the moment seemed ripe, I asked the children to visualize the night sky as they saw it on the field trip and paint 10 responses. In art school, we always had to do more than one; sometimes we did 100. I thought 10 was an appropriate number for second graders to try out various solutions.

Cathy explains to this rapt group the "work receipts" she requires each day. "Sophia wrote about the difficulties of mixing the color brown she wanted and how the next day couldn't get the same color; another day Sophia wrote about the obstacles she overcame as she learned to paint a comet." These work receipts, containing Sophia's interests, thinking, reflections, false starts, and successes, eventually find their way into her portfolio.

I am hooked, intrigued by the complex effort that has gone into combining the child's creative process with specific content and assessment. The energy in the room is high, give-and-take between teachers and researchers easy—no accident, since one theme of the effort is "Discourse Across Boundaries." Questions instantly address the connections between looking carefully at a child's work, which the group has just done, and assessing it: "Did you have a standard that you hoped Sophia would reach?" "Do you think she demonstrated understanding of the solar system?" Sophia's own standards, so beautifully expressed in her own writing about her work, are instantly juxtaposed to the external standards held by teachers and the world beyond school. Educators and policymakers everywhere face the same intricate tensions between children's standards and the world's standards.

This eight-day summer institute—convened to explore just such knotty issues—includes teachers from three collaborating national reform networks: Harvard's Project Zero, the Coalition of Essential Schools, and Foxfire. This institute is part of the Four Seasons Project on Authentic Assessment, which is in turn part of an ongoing project to reshape classroom practice and school policy. To this end, 70 participants talk to each other late at night in the dormitory, over meals, around the piano, and in small daily "home" groups. Invited researchers from the three partnerships join the extended conversations to illuminate each network's perspectives on assessment. This intense summer experience stirs up everyone's thinking ("intellectual boot camp," said one enthusiast) and sends teachers back to their own settings with, as Cathy Skowron said in her evaluation, "ideas, solutions, and more problems."

On behalf of the National Center for Restructuring Education, Schools, and Teaching (NCREST) at Teachers College, Columbia University, which coordinates this Four Seasons Project, I am charged with rendering how teachers at this institute think about assessment, how they build knowledge, and how they struggle to implement meaningful reform. These teachers have ceased to believe that standardized tests accurately measure either school effectiveness or student progress. They wrestle with questions that cut across the particulars of context: How do we know students are learning? How much and what do they have to know to reach an acceptable standard? Who decides the standards and by what right? To document their answers in their own settings, I jump at the chance to visit three geographically and ethnically diverse classrooms, one from each Four Seasons partner network: Cathy Skowron (Project Zero), Marla English and Barbara Renfrow-Baker in Seattle (Foxfire), and Millie Sanders (Coalition) in Boston.

In October 1993, when I begin, portfolios happen to be the most prominent assessment practice; another time of year exhibitions or performance assessments might engage these teachers. I am after more than a description of how these teachers use portfolios. How they think about assessment depends on their assumptions about human worth, their conceptions of how intellectual growth proceeds, and their choices about the content they teach and evaluate. Portfolios embody these choices through the details of daily classroom life and are the windows to teachers' thinking—not the reason for the story. Though I wrote the actual descriptions, these portfolio stories are "co-constructed." I observed, inquired into practice, and listened to teachers' questions. Together we worked to make their practice explicit.

Nationally, portfolio talk is in the air. To some audiences, portfolios are simple folders that hold completed work, including skills sheets; in other venues, portfolios are an elaborately refined collection of a student's best work or an extensive compilation of drafts produced along the way toward a final product. Some portfolios aim to replace standardized tests; others are designed to provoke teacher reflection, aid college admissions, or evaluate programs. Some teachers use them to provide parents, teachers, and the students themselves with evidence that students have mastered essential skills. Other portfolios are mainly an unadorned repository containing evidence of children's growth over time to be studied by the wider education community. Some portfolios encourage students to construct idiosyncratic reflections on their own learning. Others strictly dictate content. Some portfolios must be deemed reliable and valid within a district to be considered worthwhile, while teachers generate others for individual purposes.

Serious unresolved issues confront this enterprise. Some teachers grade portfolios. For others, grades are a whispered obscenity. Some teachers favor standardizing portfolios; some find it anathema. Others aren't sure. Some wonder about how much a teacher's voice should be evident in the portfolios, while others are pleased if portfolios allow for any student selection at all. Uniform answers do not serve diverse practitioners. Each of the teachers portrayed here is deeply immersed in thinking about how to assess student learning and each story differs.

The teachers in this documentation project agonize over the pressures the system brings to bear on students who do not fit some arbitrary mold, whether it be a numerical scale to measure grade-level reading or a distant standard that ignores children's diverse aptitudes and devalues their talents. Cathy Skowron, Marla English, Barb Renfrow-Baker, and Millie Sanders know that students differ and learn differently, that systemwide solutions and prescriptions don't work. They also know that explicit conventional standards have a place in schools, that expectations and standards are intertwined, and that the real world beckons with workplace requirements and academic gates.

Because these teachers value human variety in their classrooms, they care about individuals rather than universals, which forces them to grapple with the very real tension between external, conventional standards and internal, personal standards. They face times when they are held responsible for accommodating individuals—whose strengths and weaknesses they know—to unrealistic external standards imposed variously by society, upper-grade teachers, parents, standardized tests, and district, state, and national standards. To these teachers, external academic standards imply ranking, competition, and elitism, and contradict the human variety they see everyday in their classrooms. None of these schools tracks students. None of these teachers believe in tracking. All want special education students in regular classrooms with extra support. But as these teachers struggle philosophically and morally to honor the octopus of multiple standards, they have to fight the tentacle-like grip of agendas that serve some students badly. As Marla English feels "whomped" between the system and the developmental paths of children, Millie Sanders feels even more squeezed because the stakes are higher for her adolescent students. Barb Renfrow-Baker's "It depends" is a common response when she is asked to standardize a non-standard task. For humanely motivated reasons, they can live with unresolved ambivalence and half-formed answers, even when distant stakeholders may label their thinking illogical or impractical.

These teachers are caught between two definitions of standards. The Oxford English Dictionary's historical definition of standard is rooted in "the king's standard," the highly visible place on the battlefield where the king issues commands to the army. Currently that definition translates to "excellence prescribed by some acknowledged authority." But buried in antiquity, "standard" also carries a meaning of "stretching out." Students expanding their reach and their horizons to achieve what they value is a more congenial way of thinking about standards to the teachers chronicled here. As teachers bushwhack through the landscape of everyday issues with colleagues, reconciling these two definitions constitutes an unmet challenge, a permanent given of teaching and learning in the 1990s. They ask themselves relentlessly: How can we evaluate students' growth *and* hold them to standards of knowledge—especially if notions of arbitrary standards and content are flawed? They wrestle with how to combine the most fair and equitable judgments with support for individuals, and, always, the challenge of children whose pace and achievements do not match the expectations of the school system. They strive to allow for the idiosyncrasy of individual variation while at the same time insisting that children reach fundamental academic goals. They will not be distracted from the human variation in their classrooms, which paradoxically is why standards cannot be standard.

The politics of assessment joins teachers' personal values to complicate the stories. Cathy Skowron teaches second grade at the Provincetown Veteran's Memorial Elementary School (PVMES), where the initial leadership for change came from a principal in response to a national spirit of reform. Cathy's circumstance is the most straightforward and apolitical of the three contexts. PVMES teachers are not being asked, nor have they attempted, to go beyond their own school with the results of their new assessments. Parents and teachers wanted more evidence about children's progress, about what and how they were learning, and so without district pressure or urging from the school board, the faculty began to develop portfolios. In their fourth year of portfolio work, Provincetown teachers operate within a broad consensus, building on their previous learning, and going forward with their new work. Without the political pressures that assessment often brings, this case highlights how Cathy Skowron makes portfolios a valuable inquiry for children and their parents, and for their next teachers.

Marla English and Barbara Renfrow-Baker, who team teach a first/second/third-grade class in Bellevue, Washington, present a more complex scenario where external bureaucratic constraints bear down on them. The impetus for reform came from the school board, which wants numbers to evaluate the effectiveness of the language arts program. Fortunately, the assessment project as carried out by the district included extensive professional development for teachers. The tension between the opportunities for teacher inquiry and the exacting mandate for measurement that characterizes this case is similar to the press that many innovative schools across the country find themselves facing and drives home the point that teaching and learning are complex and negotiated enterprises.

As dramatic as reform is in the early grades, reform at the high school level involves radical change. Today's urban high school students have different social needs than in the past. Fenway Middle College High School has reinvented the urban high school to meet the needs of its students.

Broadening its mission beyond a narrow definition of academics to consider students' social and emotional development, Fenway struggles with
whether the changed mission serves students' future lives as thoughtful and
reflective citizens, capable of handling work and further academic preparation. Fenway has succeeded in structuring supportive environments that
help students clear many of the developmental, social, and personal hurdles
that challenge all American adolescents and block the paths of so many from
low-income, minority backgrounds. Fenway's mission stresses social and
emotional goals, understandable since many of their students have failed
in other settings. But a moral tug of war exists between the goals of their
mission, which everyone agrees they meet, and the goals of academic standards, which they have found harder to achieve. When teachers succeed in
connecting students to academics, students have a chance to graduate from
this small personalized high school and enter college on the same campus
or elsewhere. The tension between imposing academic standards of knowledge and nurturing students is constant. Portfolios here are the catalyst for
faculty to argue, to articulate their own values, and to play out their tension and ambivalence about standards. The district cares not at all what
strategies Fenway adopts, since many of Fenway's dilemmas are seen as
intractable, but the faculty cares desperately about serving students well.
Millie Sanders, a special education math teacher, offers a look at how one
teacher participates in the dialogue—both national and local—in a school
where portfolios are in their infancy and the stakes are high.

These teachers have their eyes fully on the child as they engage in the
assessment debates. Engagement matters and it matters for teachers just as
urgently as it matters for children. Energetic, thoughtful, serious teachers
have always inhabited classrooms, but the press and public have often focused on burnout and deteriorating competence. Here are teachers, leaders beyond their classrooms, who face hard questions as they refine their
practice through changes in assessment. These teachers share an extraordinary commitment to figuring out assessment issues on behalf of students
in their classes. Extend their efforts to the other teachers in Four Seasons,
multiply those efforts by teachers in other networks, and this is the stuff of
school change on a national scale.

Stories of school change are not linear or smooth. As parents, policymakers, administrators, and teachers undergoing change, we don't always
know where to cast our eye first and philosophical clarity is barely emerging. Grappling with the mundane but ever-important logistics of portfolio
management as well as the hard philosophical dilemmas of standards in the
midst of daily classroom life is an ongoing process. Portfolios are only one
entry point to figuring out what children are learning and how we know
that. No one has certain answers. These portfolios, anchored in differing

but particular contexts, are like portfolios everywhere: never final, never neatly tied together, never entirely satisfactory to all who have an interest. Portfolios as a window into human learning and school accountability are "in development." We need more philosophical clarity, more knowledge, more ability to discern without judgment.

No agreement exists among researchers, policymakers, or practitioners about standards, assessments, or portfolios, so how teachers face the messiness is part of the story. In each of these settings, teachers allow themselves, and are allowed by the hierarchy, leeway to let issues remain unresolved without forced choices. Their ongoing public discussions leave healthy room for disagreement. In all three stories, counterpoint—even dissonance—keeps the complexity of teaching and learning alive. One purpose of telling these stories is to make teachers' struggles and growing understandings accessible to parents, other teachers, policymakers, and students of teaching. As Clifford Geertz (1973) says, "No one is after a perfection of consensus, but a refinement of debate. What gets better is the precision with which we vex each other" (p. 29).

CHAPTER 1

Portfolios in Provincetown

Children and Teachers'
Continuous and Cumulative
Inquiry into Learning

At times we seemed to move too quickly into uncharted territory and at other times we seemed mired in indecision and endless semantics. I kept hoping someone would give me a map, but later found out that no one had been here before.

—Cathy Skowron

As I walk from the main street up the hill to Provincetown Veterans Memorial Elementary School, the crisp clear October air and the sun on the water are clues to why 200 applicants apply for every teaching job. Past the high school, next to the soaring Pilgrim Memorial Monument, sits an elementary school, so much a part of the community that the number of second-generation families, including at least one faculty member who attended as a child, calls into question the norms of a modern mobile society. The children know each other well; their family names repeat throughout the student body.

Another clue to the desirability of teaching here is a generous school budget. Summer resort businesses provide the tax base and the community turns out to vote yes on the school budget at every yearly town meeting. "Why should we not vote yes?" said the owner of the guesthouse where I stayed, surprised that I would even think such a thought. The budget allows small class sizes, and when enrollment is low in a given year, even by Provincetown standards, the class is still maintained. No teacher has ever been excessed. Several staff members drive an hour each way to teach here.

Usually, affluent school systems have students with affluent parents. Not so here. "Teachers are probably the top of the economic scale," speculated someone in the faculty lunchroom. Parents run the local deli, drive the trucks, catch the fish, and provide beach tow service (to rescue "those silly people who drive their cars on the sand without letting the air out of the tires first," I was told by a second grader). June parent conferences are not held, in consideration for parents already working three summer jobs or temporarily vacating their rented houses for summer tourists who pay more. One-third of the 185 pre-K–6 children are on free or reduced-fee lunch.

In this relatively pressure-free educational setting, where faculty have shared in the school's governance for years, teachers pioneered the development of portfolios to document children's learning. A visit to Cathy Skowron's classroom offers an opportunity to see how a thoughtful teacher thinks about assessment. Cathy Skowron has been teaching in this school for 18 years, first in pre-K, then kindergarten, and for the last four years in second grade. Other faculty are called by their last names, but children call Cathy by her first name—a vestige of a career begun in early childhood classrooms.[1] Her classroom contrasts sharply with other American classrooms where children are "in workbook purgatory" (Nicholls & Hazzard, 1993) and teachers transmit ready-made knowledge into children's heads. Much literature exists about classrooms like Cathy's. Many observers consider good early childhood practice for its child-centeredness, constructivist learning by doing, and emphasis on drama, art, imagination, and projects that often take place beyond the confines of the classroom.[2] Much less is said in these accounts about what constitutes good K-3 assessment. One thing is certain: Any assessment of learning must be integral to the classroom lest it become isolated and apart from the children, the teacher, and the curriculum, and so I begin by describing Cathy's classroom—where curriculum flows from children's natural surroundings and their individual and group rhythms determine how the day unfolds.

THE CLASSROOM:
BUILDING ON CHILDREN'S NATURAL RHYTHMS

I find out early that Provincetown's setting is not always as idyllic as it looks in the morning sun. "News" in Cathy's class starts at 8:05. Tom (a pseudonym, as are all children's names) begins with an eyewitness fire report: "Yesterday a man left his wood stove burning and when he came back his house was gone." Children know all about it. Greg describes the smoke and the flames; his peers listen to him, even as they wave their hands to speak, interested in how at first his mother didn't believe him. Tom lives so close he saw the deck fall down. Together on the rug in a tight circle (all except Jennifer, whose lunch money–collecting job entitles her by classroom tradition to sit in a chair for the week), children pay close attention to each other. Cathy protects each child's turn to speak, but she has no need to draw the moral from this impromptu lesson on fire safety—the children do it themselves: No one got hurt, the man had insurance (David heard this in his parents' store), and, the class agrees, no one should leave an unattended stove burning.

The class now turns with the same energy to three boats children have brought from home, a topic related to their science and social studies curriculum. Rick explains his Lego tuna boat: "You can use harpoons to catch any kind of fish, especially tuna or swordfish, or you can use the hook to catch bluefish." Bob shows his store-bought Coast Guard Boat and there ensues a provocative discussion about the Coast Guard's role of water police, hinging on the 50-mile speed limit in the water (not applicable in a boat race, Greg assures the group). Jennifer shyly holds up her sailboat, but the detailed discussion of the boat's parts, never part of my landlocked childhood, is over my head.

I am relishing children's particular knowledge of boats and fishing when David switches to two Provincetown men who drowned last week. "Over the weekend, the harbormaster found one of the bodies from the sun flickering on his watch." Again, children possess intimate knowledge. Jon volunteers that "one of my dad's friends went diving for him last week, but he didn't find the body." David adds "the boat didn't capsize; a wave washed them out of the boat, they didn't have lifejackets, and they found a bottle of rum." Then Tom recounts that two boys, age 10 and 12, and their fathers drowned in Martha's Vineyard over the long holiday weekend: "They were wearing life jackets, but it didn't help." Children quickly see that unlike the fire and the alcohol-related drowning, this tragedy has no understandable logic. Anxiety rises, and there is side-talk about loving or hating boats. For the first time, Cathy intervenes to reassure the class simply that "water can be dangerous and you have to respect it." She calms the class by invoking the safety of the everyday classroom routine. "News" is over—after 40 minutes of high-quality attention—and students move to retrieve their math books.

This shared discussion, more morbid than one would wish for young children, is undeniably fascinating to these second graders making sense of elements in their own environment. Later, Cathy tells me that such disasters are not really an everyday occurrence, but I am alerted in the first hour of my visit to how what is most on children's minds becomes the focus for this classroom. Any worthwhile assessment grows out of those relationships and that trust.

In this talk together, the children and Cathy are building on their trusting classroom community that dissolves the boundaries between the outside world and school. Their talk links the formal curriculum and children's own lives, giving these seven-year-olds the opportunity to develop their personal values and standards and to assume responsibility for their own learning. This may sound as if Cathy is totally in charge of the content of her curriculum. She is not. Cathy's curricular choices are made within Provincetown's clear-cut district guidelines. She does not have the leeway to introduce children to offbeat and controversial curricular topics, as do some primary teachers (Jervis, 1986; Nicholls & Hazzard, 1993), but she feels free to follow the children's interests as they arise.

The challenges she presents to children grow from her knowledge of subject matter (it is no accident that children's boat vocabulary is so accurate), child development, and the children in her class. Cathy attributes the ability to see children as individuals to her early childhood background and to graduate work at Lesley College in Cambridge, where she came to see knowledge as something both children and teachers construct for themselves.

Cathy is also a visual artist, a lifelong observer of her environment as a naturalist and photographer, painter, and currently a jewelry maker, and she brings her power of observation to children and their work. She understands the value of engagement from her own artistic process. In her master's thesis (Skowron, 1992), she wrote: "I realized, when I analyzed how I paint, that I work best in solitude, with no schedule or time limits. Any interruptions or noise are distracting except for music that blocks out household sounds; I become totally absorbed in my work, not even noticing time passing." She respects children's work process: "I have observed children involved in turning an idea into a tangible product. They become totally focused on their self-appointed task, experimenting with materials, persisting in finding solutions, highly resenting any interruption by peers or adults, and unaware of the flow of activities around them." She believes that "teachers need to recognize each student as an individual of value, capable of insight, feeling, and thinking, while realizing that each will have diverse responses to learning" (pp. 11–12). She lives her beliefs in her classroom, where she has been bringing assessment issues into focus for four years. Her extensive bibliography demonstrates the reading she did to arrive at these conclusions.

A Connected Curriculum

Cathy's class (and life) are all of a piece. Her own Cape Cod community, her art-making, and her teaching are interrelated. She is married to a long-time Provincetown resident. She has known the children and their families for years, currently teaching the child of the teacher next door and the grandchild of the school secretary, who herself has been there 21 years. Last Friday, on their weekly field trip, Cathy's children collected "Signs of Fall." Now a huge sunflower and various leaves are artistically displayed on a table with a high-quality magnifying lamp and an assignment to "Draw Four Things." On this week's field trip, the second grade takes the pre-K class to the same spot to collect their own signs of fall. Clutching cranberry scoops, the second graders go off hand-in-hand with the 4-year-olds. They return loaded with cranberries to make individual cranapple tarts, a recipe choice that capitalizes on their recent experience with apples. Food, Shelter, and Clothing are the second-grade lenses for schoolwide monthly units chosen by a committee of teachers; these social studies themes unite the school even more. The classroom is rich in artifacts from these past studies. Books written by last year's children are available for this year's children to read. One such book, "The Industrial Revolution," includes children's first-person accounts of their confusion, sweat, and long hours when they made and sold popcorn for the entire school in an all-day production line. (Also displayed is a certificate for the patch of rain forest they bought with the profits.) Next month, students will study Portugal, the ancestral home of many Provincetown children.

On the bulletin board are everyone's self-portraits from the first week of school. They show a range of skin colors. Despite the variation in skin tone, the 14 children and Cathy are Caucasian. Cathy reminds me that they all came to school with sun tans.

The Day Unfolds

After News is math. With little enthusiasm, if not disguised distaste for the schoolwide math curriculum put in place by a former principal, Cathy instructs the whole group for 40 minutes. After the lesson she explains the weekly tasks listed on the blackboard:

> 2 book reports
> phonics
> pattern blocks
> fall observation
> build a boat
> computer
> human body

Cathy reiterates as she introduces the week's work: "You must complete the list." Cathy's children are used to knowing in advance the general plan for the week and having some say about it. This is contrary to the usual pattern where only the teacher knows how much time is to be allotted to an activity, even though the success of children (and teachers) is often gauged by time-on-task measures. Today a child points out: "We have one less day of school but the same amount of work." Cathy says, "If you finish everything, it could show that you are getting more efficient." She explains each task. "The fall observation is about things brought from field trip. Draw four things. Don't make it up. Use the magnifying glass." In introducing the opportunity to build a boat from found materials, she reminds children of clay boats they have been making and how "last week we learned that newspapers don't make such good boats."

After her explanations, children get right to work. Some know exactly where they want to start, others sit for a minute or two before they choose where to begin this independent work. Two boys (the well-understood limit is three at a time) go immediately to the water table to build a boat, and with an unanxious use of the Exacto knife begin to cut hulls from plastic water bottles. They quickly conceptualize their boats, a result of skill and deep understanding. Two boys start with pattern blocks. Lisa begins with phonics worksheets (which some children do at home to leave more time for activities that can only be done at school). Tatania starts cutting and pasting shapes to make a human face, but changes her mind and joins the pattern-block group on the rug. Others head for the class library to choose books for their reports. There is a free and easy flow as children move about the room. No cliques are apparent; all children could find a partner if they wanted. For the rest of the two-hour morning, children work together with each other in all kinds of partnerships or alone, eat their snack when they are hungry, try out their own new ideas, listen to and watch their classmates. The content of Cathy's curriculum is broadly fixed by the district, but that does not constrain her or the children from having autonomy over the way they learn, the structure of the classroom, or the way they use their time.

Outside of the math lesson, News, and a weekly field trip, the children spend each morning working comfortably at their own pace on this weekly assigned work. In the two days I spent in Cathy's classroom, time seemed unfragmented, almost unmarked and unnoted—except for a math lesson on reading the clock. In the six-hour day, four and one-half hours were under children's own control. Children paced themselves as they moved in and out of the various tasks that Cathy proposed and chose with whom to have lunch or play during recess. Only 90 minutes were spent in groups: News, math, and a go-around after writing time. Within the formal boundaries of the school day, children have lunch, recess, and three specialists' classes during the week. Otherwise, it is the children and Cathy who determine the course of the days—when an activity has spent itself and when the children (or a particular child) need a change of pace.

Cathy orchestrates the scene from a round table where she can oversee all. She mainly works with individuals on reading and writing while she simultaneously encourages others with questions and suggestions, gently cajoling them into extending their thinking and going beyond their first effort. She also monitors the Exacto knife usage (not every teacher would allow it) in the boat-building area, the persistence of the pattern-block users, and the boys at the computer in gales of laughter over "cockatoo," a word they are matching to its picture. Two boys building one boat want her opinion on a perennial second-grade question: "If we work together, who will take it home?" And she is the audience for many unfinished sentences—Cathy, Help me . . . ; Cathy, I can't . . . , Cathy, where is . . . that stop in midsentence because, six weeks into the year, children are answering these questions for themselves.

Self-pacing is not the only support for autonomous learning. Cathy goes to some lengths to see that her students do not see school as a contest. Her class has no reading groups where children jockey for positions, or invest their energy in who is or is not in the top group. Nor does her class have workbooks to begin the conversation "What page are you on?" The classroom structure does not support a hierarchy, where some children are rewarded and others denied for either their speed in or their mastery of traditional school skills. What she values is visible in the day's details. "That's a good idea," is a frequent comment both by children and by Cathy. Children monitor each other: "You'd better mop." "When I'm finished." There is also talk about erasers: Making mistakes is just as OK as having a good idea.

After lunch (delicious Portuguese Kale soup made by the local lunchroom staff), a light rain necessitates indoor recess. Cathy is in charge of both second grades, and double the number of children in her class have a wonderful time independently choosing among Orff instruments, games, and books while she works at her desk. (Though it cuts severely into collegial time, teachers must spell each other for lunchroom and recess duty, and early morning and afternoon parking-lot duty.)

For a change of pace and scenery, Cathy decides writing should be in the spacious, well-equipped library, which happens to be empty today. Children bring their clipboards, paper, and drawing utensils, to settle companionably into beanbag chairs with their ongoing stories—mostly about Jurassic Park–inspired dinosaurs (boys) and trolls (girls)—surprisingly genderbased choices. Cathy reads a teacher's resource book on vocabulary in between children's requests for help. After an hour of engaged writing, children move to a conference table and go around to say out loud for their peers what progress they made, a strategy for further community building that also holds them accountable for their work. Tom, visibly tired and probably sick, asks "What time do we go home?" Rick reacts: "I don't want to go home," and several children agree they don't want to go home either. Back in the classroom one of the crabs is starting to molt. Cathy gathers the children for a close look, not worrying about prompt dismissal; there are no school buses in Provincetown and parents will wait for the crabs.

Greg and the Skeleton

During the second morning of my visit, Greg chooses to put together a full-size human skeleton. The skeleton belongs to the school nurse, but Cathy has arranged for it to be in her class for the study of the human body. Greg rummages through the bones, which are in a plastic tub, and asks me to help him get started. Sitting on the rug together, we pick out the fibula and the patella. The words roll easily off of Greg's tongue as he makes connection to the need for his soccer shin guards, but the next step is harder and I wonder how he is going to complete the task without an adult beside him. Observing from her seat at a nearby table, Cathy sees his potential for getting stuck and suggests he look at the articulated skeleton in the nurse's office. It's just what he needs. Once he has a sense of the size, he continues on his own. Classmates join him, linger, chat for awhile, and leave, but Greg persists. Spread out next to him and the growing skeleton, he has three books open to skeletal diagrams. An hour later every bone is in place from the the top of the skull to the ankle. Rising to the full height of his 7-year-old stature, hands on his hips with a bit of bravado, almost posing beside his accomplishment, he tells me, "I wanted to be the first to put the skeleton together and I was. Frank didn't stay, but I stayed." Cleanup demands that the skeleton be dismantled; with no hesitation he puts the bones back in the plastic tub, and lines up for lunch.

The success of Greg's learning has as much to do with the structure of Cathy's classroom and her teaching values as it does with Greg. He had a task that interested him. He had uninterrupted time and adult support if he needed it. He had control over the way he approached this task and the order in which he chose to complete his weekly work. Imagine the same activity as a timed task or done by the whole group at once; the possibility of Greg's accomplishment diminishes. Though Cathy required everyone to try this task, she knew it to be an optimal assignment for children who are builders and who operate easily in the domain of spatial awareness, one of the multiple intelligences Howard Gardner has articulated. She knows this building task also intrigues children interested in how things are put together, or those drawn to look beneath the surfaces to find underlying structures. No one else put the skeleton together as completely as Greg, but Cathy's classroom includes enough other equally valued arenas that all children can experience success. Greg happens to be motivated by being first, which seems to contradict Cathy's noncompetitive classroom stance. This same motivation to be first sometimes underlies children's need to be speedy at workbooks, but Cathy provides multiple entry points for other children to be "first" in their strong subjects. Greg would not be first at reading group work. In many classrooms, verbal/linguistic skills are the only currency, and teachers ask children like Greg to sit quietly at a desk for hours at a time in front of texts they are not ready to master. They become discipline problems rather than master builders.

BEGINNING PORTFOLIOS: A TEACHER INQUIRY

Like many classrooms that exemplify good teaching practice, Cathy's classroom highlights assessment dilemmas. Without textbooks, grade-level basal readers, letter grades, and standardized tests before the fourth grade, there is no systematic way to talk about what children are learning. Good teachers have always known intuitively how children are doing, who is stuck, and who needs more help, but the nagging feeling persists in the minds of all that if no evidence exists beyond the anecdote, children and what they learn can slip through the cracks of daily classroom life. What follows is an exploration of these assessment issues in Cathy's classroom.

What Did Greg *Really* Learn?

Greg is an emerging reader. He can decode all the words, but he wouldn't necessarily score well on any standardized pencil-and-paper measure. Anyone who watched Greg over that hour, even a glance out of the corner of a busy but observant teacher's eye, could see his pleasure, his stamina for completion, his use of the new vocabulary, his work with symmetry and text as he decoded the placement of the skeletal ribs from the book. Cathy could make such assessments. Her background in early childhood education, her long experience observing children, refined through course work at Lesley College, and her many years as a teacher, enable her to recognize children's varying responses and to provision the classroom for children's next steps. But more systematic strategies are possible to document children's learning.

Greg's assembling the skeleton was a significant learning event, the epitome of David Hawkins's (1970) "I, Thou, and It" relationship between a child, an adult, and concrete materials from the real world. But what trace is left? How is anyone going to know how Greg values this classroom activity? What did he *really* learn? What do experiences like this show in relationship to his other learning experiences? How can his teacher report this incident to his parents? What does Greg's ability to put together a human skeleton tell the principal about achievement in a teacher's classroom? What can it say about this school's accountability to the school board? Then there is the matter of national standards—and is there a world-class standard into which this study of the human body fits and to which Greg's skill is leading?

In a perfect world, teachers would be trusted to provide for children's learning without the press for measurement that grips our nation. But even if we ignore the national obsession with testing as gatekeeping and sorting, we still need better ways than standardized tests to assess Greg's learning. We need assessments most importantly for Greg, for parents, and for teachers. The principal, superintendent, school board, and White House may have reason to be interested in Greg's learning, and whether that more distant assessment is a matter for Cathy and her faculty to determine is one of the questions they debate, but it is Greg's progress that is close to Cathy's heart.

For the last four years, Cathy has been working to integrate assessment into the daily life of her classroom. Four years ago, after 15 years of teaching, Cathy was ready for new challenges. She took a leave of absence made possible by working two seven-day-a-week summer jobs. When she returned from an invigorating year off and began to teach second grade, she was ready to rethink the way she assessed children's work and to find more concrete ways to document what children learned. Chance favored her prepared mind in the form of a Provincetown Elementary School–Project Zero collaboration. It all began with the eagerness of the (then) principal to look into schoolwide portfolios as a way to assess learning.

The Need for New Assessments

In 1990, this principal declared standardized tests useless to K–3rd graders and their teachers. The absence of the tests provoked both teachers and parents to wonder what their children were learning. Thus the need for new assessments arose both from a desire on the part of the principal and the faculty to get below the surface of standardized tests and their need to demonstrate to parents what children were learning from this new curriculum. Assessments were not developed for district accountability or as a lever for broad structural and organizational changes. In a setting relatively free from outside bureaucratic and financial pressures, this faculty pioneered the development of portfolios. Developing portfolios provided an opportunity for teachers to grapple with hard-to-figure-out attributes of children's learning, and bring that understanding to their teaching. This effort demonstrated the virtue of assessment as inquiry, not assessment as measurement (Chittenden, 1991).

The Project Zero Connection

The exploration of portfolio assessment began when several Veterans Memorial Elementary School faculty heard Howard Gardner speak and came away intrigued with the theory of multiple intelligences and the accompanying portfolio work. They encouraged the principal to contact Project Zero, an educational research organization co-directed by Howard Gardner and David Perkins, based at Harvard Graduate School of Education. Project Zero comprises many separate components, but since 1984, one of them has been working with schools willing to think about assessment (Seidel & Walters, 1994). In 1990 they were looking for another school to begin a new collaboration. The timing was right; both Project Zero and Veterans Memorial agreed to the match, and they have been thinking together ever since about new ways to assess children's learning.

The school change agenda brought by the principal and Project Zero encouraged this faculty to consider new options for getting at what was happening with students in their classrooms. Cathy recounted her version: "The development of portfolios came out of all the work we did with curriculum over 15 years—we knew we couldn't tap the deep skills kids had with any kind of testing, standardized or otherwise. We knew we weren't getting all we could. My impetus was to validate kids' voices." To institute portfolios schoolwide where no portfolios exist is hard work. Cathy regards the collaboration of Project Zero as essential in this effort.

In 1990–1991, Project Zero staff came to Provincetown. Among the Four Seasons partners, Project Zero alone is primarily a research effort. Foxfire is a network of teachers working for reform, individual teacher by individual teacher, and the Coalition for Essential Schools concerns itself with system-wide school change; both Foxfire and the Coalition propose common understandings that unite their members' efforts. Unlike those who join Foxfire or the Coalition, the Provincetown faculty did not commit itself to any such codified set of principles or practices, only to a spirit of inquiry in figuring out, as Cathy tells her children, "how to prove what you have learned." Project Zero documented the work at Provincetown Elementary and asked questions of the faculty to clarify teachers' thinking. A Project Zero handout summarizes the first two years as "focused on designing and creating portfolios that were accurate and compelling records of a child's classroom work."

Looking at Children and Their Work

Project Zero puts high value on attention to children's work, an attitude they brought to Provincetown in the form of the Collaborative Assessment Conference (CAC). The Collaborative Assessment Conference is a process that ensures that teacher talk about children is divorced from negative judgments that often float unchecked through faculty rooms without regard for the strengths of students. CAC sessions focus on student work, rather than teaching practice. Teachers are asked to follow guidelines designed to elicit serious attention to the work being presented to the group. Colleagues look at the work in silence and then each, uninterrupted, addresses the following questions: (1) What is most striking to you about this project? (2) What questions do you have about the work and about its creator when you look at it? (3) What evidence do you have that the work is of genuine importance to the student? (4) What inferences might you draw about this student's interests, curiosity, or strengths? Participants are asked to support their comments with references to the work itself, which increases their ability to observe, to describe what they see, and to talk about work without judging it. Among the tasks of CAC are to discuss what next steps the student is ready for and to think about what kind of feedback might be given to the student and in what form. Though it is not necessary to assess by portfolios in order to learn by observing and describing student work, one of the important purposes of portfolios is related to that careful looking. Indeed, learning to look at a child's work in relation to the child is a compelling reason for collecting the work in the first place.

Cathy has always done this close observation naturally as a corollary to her own art-making, and it came to the fore when she was thinking about the creative process in her master's degree work. Several years ago, after her class studied the solar system, looked at Van Gogh's *Starry Night,* and took a night field trip, she asked them to do 10 paintings in response, a classic art school exercise but rarely done by second graders. In her master's thesis (Skowron, 1992), Cathy documented two children's very different approaches to this assignment (pp. 30–56). Cathy and Project Zero often use the resulting art in workshops to demonstrate how describing children's work can enhance practice and how withholding judgment and talking about what is actually on the page helps teachers to know individual children better and plan for their learning. It was this art work and Cathy's intriguing comments about it at the 1993 Four Seasons Summer Institute that first drew me to her classroom.

Stewing, Muddling, and Working It Through

During that first year (1990–1991), Project Zero gave three workshops for the whole faculty. In addition, throughout the year each teacher was paired with a colleague—a critical friend with whom to share feedback and commiserate when the work stalled. Project Zero staff came each month to visit classrooms and consult with these pairs of teachers. At the end of the school day, the Project Zero staff and any teachers who wanted to would retire to Napi's, a local restaurant, to hash out the philosophy and mechanics of portfolios. The Project Zero staff took notes, which they circulated back to the faculty. This feedback gave teachers needed direction as they went along. Teachers did not necessarily agree with each other on how to "do" portfolios or even on the principles behind them. No one had a predetermined kind of portfolio in mind. Cathy says, "I spent a whole year wondering why we had to do the exercises Project Zero kept giving us. We thought they must have known the answers and more than once wished Project Zero would have just told us. But no one had the answers."

Trying to implement portfolios across the whole curriculum that year seemed too daunting, so each teacher took a curricular area and began to look at what kind of work was collectible and what could be done with it. They reviewed work with children and presented these incipient portfolios at parent conferences, with good response.

As the faculty got deeper into what it means to assess learning, they tackled larger projects. Encouraged by their progress with parents and children over the 1990–1991 school year, they formed a committee, on which Cathy served, to work during the summer of 1991. This group wrote a compendium of their thinking in a handbook for teachers entitled *Portfolio Assessment Using a Multidimensional Approach to Evaluating Student Learn-* (Provincetown Faculty, 1991). Called more familiarly *The Portfolio Handbook*, it lays out their philosophical vision, drawing heavily from Elliot Eisner: Education ought to promote the exploration of ideas, lead to a better, more satisfying life outside of school, move away from extraneous reward systems, and engage children in formulating their own problems to solve. Further, educators should engender a tolerance for ambiguity and provide opportunities for children to express their imaginings. "Multidimensional" refers to Howard Gardner's multiple intelligences and his recommendations are also included: Emphasize regular assessment rather than testing; integrate assessment and learning; devise assessment that peers directly into the intelligence in operation rather than mediating it through language and logic; be sensitive to individual differences and forms of expertise; and undertake assessment primarily to aid students. This handbook, now in a three-ring binder, has in it a definition of what this faculty means by a portfolio: "a careful and conscious collection of student's work which provides a multidimensional picture of a student's learning over time, accounts for both process and products, and includes the active participation of students in their own learning."

The bulk of the handbook is given over to examples of student work along with the schemes teachers have devised for assessing them. Honoring diverse practice, the handbook contains work scored numerically by the teacher in one classroom next to work assessed by children from another. No agreement on the details was necessary or expected.

This faculty committee realized in its second year that collecting student work by subject failed to capture important individual learning, and since that was the goal, they revised their procedures. In a major switch away from a curricular lens, the committee decided to organize their work around children rather than content. Cathy remembers vividly how the teachers developed a "humongous" list of essential elements they wanted in any profile of student learning. They winnowed the list down to what the faculty held in common and those attributes make up the four "dimensions of learning" (see following section). From this year of stewing, muddling, and working through the process of characterizing learning, the committee produced a systematic piece of work.

Dimensions of Learning: An Evolving Structure for Portfolios

Four years after Project Zero began in Provincetown, the faculty arrived at the structural centerpiece of the school's portfolio assessment. This work, now a revised section in the *Portfolio Handbook*, is called *The Dimensions of Learning.* "*Dimensions,*" as both children and adults refer to it, stipulates a framework for positioning children's work next to a standard. It is here that the teachers focused on the relationship between the learning process and the curriculum. For a start, the handbook says, "A *dimension* is a characteristic which describes an aspect of the nature and scope of learning."

Dimensions provides a common language for guiding dialogues with children about their learning, guidelines for collecting work samples, and a multifaceted lens for assessing learning. *Dimensions* also specifies the criteria the faculty developed for whether a child meets the standard. There are four separate dimensions. One of the four, Acquisition and Application of Knowledge, has always been addressed in schools by report cards, and the user of this framework is invited to refer to the Provincetown curriculum guides, which "articulate the appropriate concepts, information, processes, and skills." Another dimension is Communication, which includes a standard for written work, oral reports, projects (construction, dioramas, etc.) and performances (drama, music, etc.) where the emphasis is on effective presentation of information, ideas, and/or feelings. Attitudes and Approaches attempts to describe the process of learning to learn, the stance children take toward their work. Newer to the assessment debate is the dimension of Reflections, an effort to make children conscious of their own learning processes.

Attitudes and Approaches—"a collection of behaviors and proclivities that characterize the ways in which a child engages in learning"—provoked the most discussion. The faculty knew they had to capitalize on individual attitudes and approaches to help children develop their abilities. Cited here as an example of a child's thinking about his learning process is a 7-year-old's letter addressed to his next year's teacher: "I concentrate and sometimes I work alone so I just get it done without someone asking me questions. I like to work with someone when a thing is hard. We are not copying, but we work together like one mind." Following this child's insightful comment is a list of 20 behaviors that the faculty agreed exemplify attitudes and approaches. Among the 20 are: easily engages in activity, shows persistence, takes risks, adopts effective behaviors modeled by others, takes a deliberate and thoughtful approach, uses past knowledge and experiences, and completes tasks in a timely fashion. Under each of these behaviors are indicators that further delineate what adults and children might look for as they consider whether children possess these attitudes and approaches. "Using thinking abilities to solve problems, make decisions, and examine issues" may be the least controversial. It is the most complete. The bulleted list includes:

- Shows interest in problem posing and/or issue examination.
- Shows interest in problem solving and/or decision-making.
- Uses various problem-solving and/or decision-making strategies.
- Collects data from a variety of sources.
- Gathers data in a variety of ways.
- Asks questions.
- Seeks evidence.
- Seeks alternatives.
- Evaluates alternatives critically.
- Shows evidence of fluency, flexibility, originality, and elaboration.
- Generates answers and solutions.
- Carries out plans.

"Sustains Focus" has a shorter list:

- Child demonstrates an intensity in activity and use of materials.
- Child attends to work despite surrounding distractions (this goes beyond straightforward interest; focus indicates an usual attention, singularity of purpose on the part of a child.)

Under "Shows Seriousness" are these items:

- Child's approach to task is straightforward.
- Child can be serious and show enjoyment at the same time.

While they developed these dimensions, teachers raised the hard question of what is measurable and what is not. When they attempted to develop a scoring mechanism for Attitudes and Approaches, they ran into trouble. Cathy felt strongly: "As relevant to children's learning as attitudes are, you can't score them," and her view prevailed. Even when teachers agreed that scoring attitudes and approaches was unwise, teachers found some student characteristics particularly hard to think about in a conversation about measurement. Sense of humor is nowhere on the list. Teachers talked. They argued. They compromised. Some teachers thought the ability to work quietly was important; others wanted to recognize children who need to talk through their learning. Both criteria appear paradoxically side by side in this new document.

The teachers concluded that the use of the four dimensions "results in a portfolio of the child's work that provides a broad and in-depth picture of the child." Their *Portfolio Handbook* is a written, public compilation of their joint thinking. So impressive is this faculty effort that the school is informally selling it to interested buyers.

That year teachers also arrived at the notion of benchmarks—entry, midpoint, and exit levels—to guide them in thinking about what students should know, understand, and be able to do. They began to explore together how these benchmarks related to report cards. The unresolved debate about how to judge whether children's work compares to benchmarks goes on to this day. The form and purpose of the report cards are "in transition," especially as parents learn more and more about their children from the portfolios. Faculty know that report cards without benchmarks do not answer the parent's question about how children are doing compared with other children and a grade-level standard, even as they acknowledge that grade level is an artificial invention of textbook manufacturers and testmakers. This issue of benchmarks and report cards is still one of the issues, as Cathy says, "mired in indecision and endless semantics."

The *Portfolio Handbook* is a document generated by a particular group of teachers; another faculty might value different criteria or state standards differently. But no matter what the final document looks like, implicitly embedded in any such discussion are enduring questions that teachers rarely talk about with colleagues: What are the purposes of education? What is the nature of teaching? What constitutes learning? Even when teachers hold competing values, through talking they make their practice explicit to themselves and each other. Assessment forums serve many needs, but among the most important are continuing conversations. When teachers put language to what they do in the classroom, the conversation informs their practice and sharpens what they see. In turn, sharpened vision improves the ability to articulate assumptions, which improves practice, putting in place and reinforcing a hard-to-beat cycle of professional growth.

Although Cathy can emphasize what is most useful to her about the dimensions, and downplay what doesn't fit with her beliefs, she is committed to implementing staff agreements about portfolios—for instance, how the dimensions will relate to these collections of work, how big the pass-along portfolio will be, and whether any requirements will be expected. So far none of what she must do in her classroom to honor these agreements conflicts with her own teaching practice. This congruence between staff consensus and her own values is due, perhaps, to her own intimate involvement with the development of these portfolios. Further, as the *Portfolio Handbook* shows, contradictions in teaching practice can live side by side; the document is an artifact to be revisited later, when thinking has changed. The faculty are basically in agreement with the direction portfolios have taken and the pace at which they have been implemented. She and her colleagues "own" these portfolios.

In response to a draft of this paper and my request, Cathy wrote a description of portfolios in her classroom, recording her early experiences with portfolios and how she uses them now. Cathy describes portfolios as "a four-year road of discovery," and goes on to highlight her feelings as a pioneer:

> At times we seemed to move too quickly into uncharted territory and at other times we seemed mired in indecision and endless semantics. I kept hoping someone would give me a map, but later found out that no one had been here before. We reflected on our teaching practices, we worked with colleagues, we consulted researchers, and we enlisted children as collaborators to discover what we might mean by portfolio assessment. For me, the story developed simultaneously in each of these arenas.
>
> It is now four years later. Exciting innovations, experiments, agreements, disagreements, and revisions have resulted in the evolution of portfolio practice in my classroom. Howard Gardner's theory of multiple intelligences remains the philosophical underpinning. Our *Dimensions of Learning* remains the framework for collecting and assessing student work. The original purpose of portfolios was to document individual student learning over time. I think it has broadened to become a portrait of each child. The portfolio collection now tries to answer the question for each child, "Who are you?"

IMPLEMENTING PORTFOLIOS:
AN INQUIRY WITH CHILDREN

In good progressive classrooms (today and in the past) teachers often preside over lively project-based activities and then discuss with children the quality of their work. But such discussion—less systematic and more impressionistic than the reflective talk that goes on in Cathy's classroom—does not, nor did it ever, occupy the central place that Cathy gives it. In addition to exposure to integrated subject matter, autonomous self-pacing, and life in a democratic community, children are being consciously and conscientiously taught a new way of thinking about their learning. Their experience with continuous, cumulative self-reflection that Cathy has described is new to the assessment dialogue.

Dimensions in the Classroom

As a result of her portfolio work, Cathy is ever aware of opportunities to capture what children know and how they go about knowing it. Whenever teachers pay careful attention to children's work, they deepen their understanding of their own practice, but in addition, Cathy's practice is designed to deepen children's understanding of their own learning. Cathy's goal is to ask her students to assess themselves on all kinds of implicit and explicit criteria (the *Dimensions* document includes both) and to make what happens in her classroom visible both to herself and to the children. In explaining how she accomplishes this job, she begins with classroom organization. From her written description:

> In my classroom, each child has a personal space with a folder for collecting samples of learning from each term. I use a cardboard cubby system. What is collected in these cubbies and folders? Each child has a cassette tape to record oral reading at least once a year to document developing ability. These are passed to me from previous teachers and I will pass them on to next year's teacher.
>
> Students use "work receipts, " a system I developed to keep track of work that often has no written record, as part of the documentation of their daily learning. Children save their week's work along with their work receipts until Friday, when we set aside time to reflect on them. On Friday children fill out weekly reflection sheets, which provide in their own voices a record of what they have done for the week [see Figure 1.1]. These weekly reflection sheets go in children's term portfolios. In addition, each portfolio has a checklist with the *Dimensions* on it and by the end of the term children must include something for each dimension and check it off.

The long-term task includes an introduction to the language of assessment. In September, Cathy asks children to brainstorm this question: "How can you prove you have learned something?" By presenting this question

G R e g

End of Week Reflection

What was your <u>best</u> work this week? Why?

Re ad i n g   c ou se I l i Ke to
re ad

(Reading because I like to read)

What was most difficult? Why?

b ook re por t cos te
I c a n no t ever get t hem
done   (book report because I cannot
ever get them done)

One goal for next week is

t o ge t ou r W or K do ne
b y t use da y

(to get our work done by Tuesday)

What is your plan?

t o n o t foo l a r on d

(to not fool around)

FIGURE 1.1 Greg's End of the Week Reflection for 9/24

as a problem to solve together, she encourages children to take responsibility for their own learning. Children typically list: write it down, tell someone, make something, use video, computers, photographs. "I encourage kids to use a variety of documentation methods and I remind them frequently of the possibilities." This first discussion gives children concrete ideas about how to begin an inquiry into their own learning that will continue throughout the year:

As students gain experience with the process and vocabulary of portfolio assessment, they learn to apply criteria to their learning. As the year goes on and I sense that children are ready to go beyond the answers "this is my best work because I liked it," or "it was fun," I teach specific lessons on the criteria to meet each dimension. Samples of children's weekly reflections show how they apply these criteria to their learning."

When I ask Cathy to talk more about how she uses the dimensions in her classroom, she says, "I keep the dimensions in my head all the time." After a pause, she muses, "If you believe in something, you work out of your head all the time," and then asks herself rhetorically, "but how do I work from my head?" Putting language to this knowledge that governs teachers' actions is where intuition joins craft. Cathy—like all teachers—has deep intuitive knowledge about her teaching, but rarely are teachers asked to talk about practice, so knowledge remains, as Cathy says, "in my head." I am asking Cathy to make her tacit knowledge explicit. She responds, "Some of what I do is so personally part of me that I am unaware of knowing it."

Cathy acknowledges that *Dimensions* is the most systematic portfolio work done by the faculty. As a result, its criteria and standards frame what Cathy notices in her classroom world. She readily agrees that for her the dimensions that concern the process of learning are more prominent than those concerning products. She provides an example of how she used *Dimensions* language with children: When three children built a haunted house out of blocks, they made up a skit without words accompanied by "spooky music" on a portable keyboard and performed it for the class. She asked the audience, "How did you know what you saw?" Children could tell what was happening by the action and they "got" the music. Cathy then talked about the Communication dimension and how this skit met its standard for clarity. She adds another case: "When kids say, 'I want to work with someone who doesn't fool around,' I have the dimension of Attitude and Approach in mind. I ask, 'Well, how do you know who to pick?'" *Dimensions*, she feels, has given her a framework for seeing and a broader vocabulary for conversing with children about their learning.

Cathy not only talks about the use of language in articulating her own knowledge, but she consistently returns to this theme with children. Knowing how to talk explicitly about one's practice is as valuable for students as for teachers. "Putting language to practice," as Cathy says, is central for her. She uses the language of *Dimensions* when she reviews children's work with them, and encourages them to name the evidence that supports their efforts to meet the standards of the four dimensions. She has a pattern: "I focus on certain dimensions certain times of year. I put the lists on an overhead. I help until kids get fluent."

Cathy cites how Sven gained skill and control when he stood up before the whole school in a mock town meeting (the Provincetown form of town governance) to propose an amendment to an article on cleaning up the beaches. Cathy helped him to see that the standard for effective communication in this setting demanded practice to reduce his nervousness so he could say what he wanted without hesitation. "It was too important to mess up," he finally recognized. The *Dimensions* language supported his learning. Toward March, April, and May, children really begin to use the *Dimensions* language fluently.

More tangible evidence of children's engagement with assessment comes from the work receipts children complete daily. Work receipts are Cathy's device for children to keep track of their own learning, especially when their work leaves behind no product. They are also public documents that represent students' evolving and negotiated understanding of standards and how to reach them. On a one-page sheet, children answer questions about their work: "What did you do?" "How did you do it?" "What did you learn?" and have it signed by a witness, either a student or a teacher. Then, each Friday morning children spend time looking through these work receipts and other work they have done and pull pieces for their term portfolio. During this time they fill out the two-sided weekly reflection sheet, which includes a list of disciplines on one side. Cathy confers with each child to determine whether their work falls into art, computer, exercise, math, music, reading, science, social studies, or writing. She encourages children to pick a portfolio piece for each discipline. Turning over the sheet, children record answers to: "What was your *best* work this week? Why? What was the most difficult? Why?" They write one simple goal for the following week and a plan for reaching it. Cathy uses these questions to introduce the language of quality and goal setting into children's vocabulary. Setting goals and reflecting on quality, she believes, are important components of lifelong learning.

In my two-and-a-half-day October visit, I did not hear a lot of this kind of assessment talk with children. Cathy explained: "Children need more experience thinking about their learning before I begin to introduce specific assessment language for them to consider. October is too early."

In answer to my question about where children express their own values, Cathy answers that the four dimensions are sufficient to cover most of what children value as well as what teachers value. "They are a quick guide for them as they are for us. Kids can find themselves."

Assessing Greg's Learning: A Portfolio in Action

When Greg finished his skeleton, Cathy was on the spot immediately with a camera to document this complex piece of second-grade science work. She regrets she has no video and explains the classroom use of the camera. She writes:

> A major deletion from my practice is the use of video documentation. Time to tape, budget constraints (children all had their own tapes), equipment management, and viewing logistics contributed to its demise. I still think, however, that video documentation is the best way to capture evidence of the whole child. For documentation I now rely more on photos accompanied by children's written descriptions. During the week a child or I can request a photo of some learning that seems significant, or on Friday a child can ask me to photograph work which seems important in retrospect. Later, with photos in hand, students describe in writing what is important about that work and together we figure out what we can learn about them from the photo and the description. Often students will dictate part of their responses to photos, especially if I am asking them open-ended questions to clarify or expand their thinking. As one of my eight-year-olds once said, "I can think better than I can read or write."

Greg could have initiated the request for a picture or Cathy might have initiated it, but this moment with the bones was so clear to both of them that when Cathy got out her camera, Greg was ready to be photographed. Cathy's ever-ready camera is a result of her belief that children are sometimes too young to realize the significance of what they have done. If she values an experience by taking a photo, children realize its importance. This moment of teacher-student interaction also becomes an opportunity for reflective discussion. Cathy can instruct in the criteria for a good job. "I can discuss with kids what does 'best work' mean? what is 'difficult work' and is there a difference? How do you know the difference?"

As children begin to see patterns in their work, they realize that their successes are not random accidents. Since they can control their work process—how they begin, when they take breaks, whom they ask for help, how they handle false starts—they come to understand themselves as learners. With this understanding, they develop confidence in their ability to repeat their successes on other occasions. Children can also recognize what processes and work habits are most useful, which gives them power over how they proceed with classwork. In a classroom where the teacher dictates and times the way work is accomplished, children have no chance to learn these lessons.

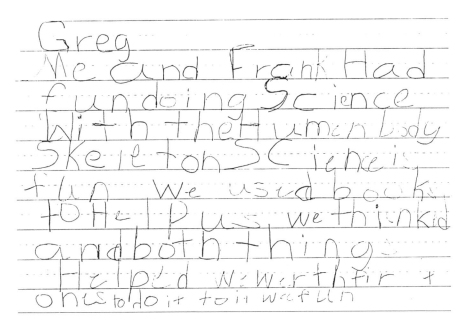

FIGURE 1.2 Greg and his completed skeleton

On a Friday morning, when a batch of photos (including Greg's) came back from developing, students wrote what they thought was significant about their pictures. Cathy elaborates: "Before this photo goes into Greg's term portfolio—either by his choice or mine or both—I will interview him to find out more." Cathy used what she observed the day he formed the skeleton to probe Greg's thinking in an interview. She noted that Frank had helped Greg even more than Greg remembered or admitted. She also saw that Greg had difficulty figuring out the proper placement of the ribs from the two-dimensional charts in the books. From these observations she knows that Greg will need more experience making use of written schematic information and that he will have to think more about crediting peers. Totally engaged in the actual skeleton, Greg is less interested in writing than Cathy would like. It is a challenge to her to entice Greg to write down his reflections, but she regards this reflective writing as important as the original activity. Using the photo to prompt his writing, Cathy sat with him while he wrote (see Figure 1.2).

Greg ultimately wrote how much fun he had and repeated three times how much he likes science. Greg also acknowledged (with Cathy's prompting) the help he had from Frank and reminded the reader that he was the first to finish and that he worked *hard*. He then put the attached writing and the photo into his interim portfolio folder. Taken alone, this writing by a struggling writer may not show Greg's excitement and engagement or convince an outsider that this activity with the bones was worthwhile learning. However, one piece of work does not stand alone in a portfolio. Later, when a decision is made about whether this piece will go in his term portfolio, more evidence and context will be available.

Good teaching practice and good curriculum development emerge from the essential triad of a child's interests, subject matter, and teacher. When Cathy read an early draft of this paper, it prompted her to relate a recent incident with Greg that shows how this triad works as she builds on Greg's interest in bones. The math book (really not so bad, she says on this occasion) had some work on platonic solids, including pictures of pyramids and dodecahedrons. Greg's interest led her to borrow another teacher's construction kit. Greg put every shape together and learned the tongue-twisting vocabulary. Cathy believes both his skill and his pleasure should show up in his portfolio (see Figure 1.3). She notes that bones will appear again in January during the paleontology unit on dinosaurs, but she knows that other related topics will arise around Greg's interests. Cathy did not ask Greg to think about his bone work in relation to the dimensions. "It was too early." Later she may ask the whole class to look at what Greg wrote in October and ask, "What can we learn about Greg as a student from his writing about the skeleton?"

Greg

Me and Casey and Robert bilt an Icostahedron It was sord hard. it took us ahalfan hour or more. We stuck with it. I am Proud that we got It done.

FIGURE 1.3 Greg and his colleagues with their platonic solids

One example of a child's use of a dimension, work receipt, or weekly reflection sheet may show something relevant about the learner, but the power of these individual items is cumulative. By January, Cathy thinks children are more thoughtful when they write about their learning—they notice patterns in their choices, their efforts at problem solving, their difficulties, and their areas of improvement. Again, Cathy emphasizes that teaching children the language is important; when they know the language, they can articulate the criteria that match the standards. Then they have more power and control over their own learning.

The End of the Year: More Than a Folder

At the end of the year, Cathy tells me, children look back over their three term portfolios and prepare their "pass-along portfolios" to take with them to the next teacher. Portfolios mavens are always interested in who chooses the work for these permanent records—children or teachers. In her written description, Cathy makes it clear that portfolios in her classroom are a negotiated process:

> Although I require some types of work, the child has the final say about which piece is or isn't included. We might negotiate on a particular piece. Usually we differ because they think something isn't good enough or they resist putting a first draft in when I see their progress and they don't, but we reach agreement before including it. Toward the year's end we begin culling the term portfolio for the pass-along portfolio. As the children look through their collections, discussion centers around the balance between enough and too much. I ask each child to answer the question, "Who are you? What do you want someone, specifically your parents and next year's teacher, to know about you?" Children look back on previous and the current portfolios. Much self-discovery takes place and each child's portrait begins to emerge for the pass-along portfolio. Each child writes a letter of introduction to accompany the portfolio.

I looked at the pass-along portfolios compiled by her last year's second graders (now in third grade). Each portfolio includes a *Dimensions* checklist so that children can keep track of work that demonstrates each of the four dimensions. To show evidence of Attitudes and Approaches, children include weekly reflection sheets. To show evidence of Acquisition and Application of Knowledge, children include evidence from each subject area. To demonstrate Communication, children include one or more examples of written work and evidence of oral presentations, projects, and performances. To demonstrate the dimension of Reflection (both immediate and long-term), children include some weekly reflection sheets and reflective writing they do over the year and writing or drawings they do in June after they have looked through the year's work.

In the portfolios are required letters to the next teacher, self-portraits from the first week of school (art), many self-chosen photographs with children's explanations attached (different for each child and each discipline—most disciplines are covered here), photos such as "What I Want People to Know About Me" (Attitude and Approaches), drafts of an illustrated story on Bank Street Writer (writing), self-chosen artifacts from field trips (social studies and science), and a reflection on their June Reading Project. This last item is unclear and Cathy reminds me that no folder of work can capture the depth and complexity of what actually happens in the classroom.

She explains that last year, children's task for the June Reading Project was to figure out some way of transforming their favorite book of the year into a performance, an art project, or a book report. After children completed their projects and performed or demonstrated them, Cathy began the assessment process. She hung the "Criteria for Reflection" from the *Dimensions* on the classroom easel and children put a blank piece of paper on their clipboards. Then she asked children to write assessments of their projects or performances, comparing their own work to the criteria for meeting a standard. For instance, children noticed that their performance exemplified clear communication because they had a diorama to display or children laughed at the funny parts of their skits. For two hours, her second graders, clipboards in hand, engaged in this high-level thinking about the quality of their own work and the elements that went into their judgments. This opportunity for children to assess their own work is a culminating occasion to practice the language of reflection, to think hard about quality, and to compare their own work with external standards. From start to finish, the June Reading Project, Cathy wearily recalls, took weeks to accomplish. But she does not regret any part of it, nor does she doubt that this long process is useful for children's growth as they refine their ability to assess themselves. Nor does she doubt its contribution to her own understanding of individual children and how they learn.

After returning to their term portfolios in a major portfolio review and selecting one or more pieces from each subject to go in their pass-along portfolios, the children's final task is to write a letter about what they would like their next teacher to know about them. They also write an end-of-the-year long-term reflection on learning, including a prompted drawing: "Self-Portrait of How I Learn Best." Children offer insights into how they learn from peers, both from others' ideas and from having an audience for their own ideas. Some recognize their own growth, and many mention that they need to work harder. By the end of second grade, Manuel (chosen at random) has a good sense of himself as a learner. He says he is a slow writer, needs to expand his friendship circle, likes to do oral presentations better than written ones, and has learned left and right from working on Logo, a computer program. He adds a meticulously drawn picture of himself working at a table with others.

Cathy writes about the uses of this pass along portfolio:

> We use this portfolio to provide parents with specific evidence of their child's learning and provide accountability to back up report cards. Teachers use the pass-along portfolio to plan the child's classroom program. The evidence is right there for portfolio readers—parents, next teachers, outside readers—to notice patterns of what children choose to do in class, their strengths and difficulties, their ways of working, their goals and how they plan for the future, but children's self-learning is key.

Not all the uses of portfolios show in the actual portfolio folder. To support the full-scale sixth-grade graduation exit exhibitions that the school instituted last year and not leave all the preparation to the sixth-grade teachers, Cathy began public "portfolio practice exhibitions" in her second grade. In order to put children at ease with the task, each child chose a friend to stand with in front of the class to offer moral support and help present the evidence. Each child talked about several pieces of work culled from the K–2 portfolios. This presentation demonstrates what they have learned and what they noticed about themselves as learners. This new effort, which could also be considered an exhibition of portfolios, is one more opportunity to instill confidence and to deepen the children's thinking about themselves as learners.

Growth Over Time: Mysterious and Elusive

Beside the benefits to teachers' own learning and the stimulus to activities that go on in individual classrooms, these portfolios provide a record of children's growth over time, but what can't be told in any standard way is the mysterious story of individual human growth. Greg volunteered to show me his pre-K, kindergarten, and first-grade portfolios, even though this delayed the start of his bone work. He took me down to the supply room where three years of portfolios are stored in old recycled cardboard boxes labeled "Cumulative Student Portfolios." They are meant to be removed for study. Teachers usually keep their current students' portfolios in their classrooms, but Greg's happened to be in this central location because his last year's teacher had recently used it for a workshop. Back in the classroom, Greg and I sat on the rug and listened to the tape of his kindergarten teacher interviewing him, and a first-grade tape of him reading from a basal. Though we enjoyed looking at the many photos and other memorabilia, much in the portfolio appeared to me as exactly that, partly since little evidence of context of the work appears and the apparatus that supports the *Dimensions* lens is not particularly visible to an outsider. In a few minutes, however, I knew that Greg was a builder from photo after photo of him in the block corner, not always with constructions of his own making. He had one spaceship story with many drafts to represent his early writing process, but it was not possible to trace his developing interests as a writer (or reader) over years. As an outsider, I got a flavor of his curriculum and a glimpse of Greg in the classroom, but many items were neither self-initiated nor particularly illuminating about Greg.

I also saw how Greg's three previous teachers managed portfolios in their classrooms. Collecting significant samples of children's work in a portfolio, organizing them sensibly, and storing them in a way that outside readers can understand is a considerable feat that takes more years to accomplish than Greg's teachers had had at that point. Greg was in kindergarten the first year of Provincetown's portfolio effort and his portfolio represents a beginning, a three-year inquiry for teachers. These early impressive efforts are still on their way to meeting Project Zero's standard of a "compelling and accurate record of a child's work." It is important to remember here that portfolios are a process in teachers' lives; the actual portfolios are only an iceberg tip of what teachers learn by designing and using them in their classrooms. It will take more time—time measured in years—to embed portfolios in daily school life so that teachers can reflect on children's learning and see the results of that inquiry in their classrooms. Looking at portfolios over time may help teachers know what children find meaningful and how individual learning unfolds.

One of the moving moments I experience looking through the boxes of cumulative portfolios is seeing the obvious breakthroughs in children's work, when they begin to have more insight, when their writing all of a sudden takes account of conventions, and when their passions show through. Miraculously, without explanation, these breakthroughs occur at different times for different children, reminding me that much about human learning and how it happens cannot be captured at any one point in time. Codified standards applicable to all cannot measure the personal standards and passions children bring to their work.

Patricia Carini (1991) in *Images and Immeasurables* uses a powerful metaphor to capture this thought. She images "a yardstick or twelve inch

ruler . . . physically rigid, marked off in exact graduated increments, pro-
scribing a linear sequence of standard units," to describe the narrow measurement routinely foisted on children when adults are seduced into these
comparisons (p. 2). She asks how that rigid rule can measure what is essentially immeasurable: "The big questions which impel humans to seek and
make knowledge . . . the world of human works . . . filled with our conflict-
ing wills and passions" (p. 5).

Although it is tempting in the presence of these cumulative portfolios
to think about comparing different children across the same time frame,
measuring children against each other cannot do any individual child
justice. Yet standards of knowledge that schools and society attempt to
impose invite these comparisons as well-intentioned educators strive for
excellence, accountability, and a well-prepared world-class work force. But
often the most valuable measurements of students' learning and growth are
not comparable.

Capturing Facility with Language

The quest to uncover children's linguistic progress often induces teachers
to isolate this elusive miracle and pin it down like a butterfly for study. The
most intriguing piece in Cathy's third-grade portfolios spoke to the question of how to capture a 7-year-old's facility with language. Each portfolio
had a different typed version of the *Legend of Sleepy Hollow*, with handwritten drafts attached. As an outside reader, I saw only a standard entry sheet
that said: "We listened to three versions of the *The Legend of Sleepy Hollow*
and wrote it down. It took _____ minutes to complete," with the number
filled in for each child. Cathy and I wonder how much context about a piece
of work is useful to later readers. The teacher's voice here may be too little
evident, but how not to drown out children's voices with the teachers' voices
is one of Cathy's issues.

Although Cathy sometimes worries that she puts too much emphasis in
portfolios on products and not enough on process, the *Legend of Sleepy
Hollow* retellings capture both the children's learning process and her own.
Cathy's description of how this piece came to be demonstrates her evolving portfolio practice, her trial-and-error effort to document children's learning, and how both are infused with the spirit of inquiry. I took this description from an informal interview:

> I kept hearing the first grade teacher talk about how useful it is to
> repeat things and I know kids like it. So last year when it was near
> Halloween and I had several versions of Washington Irving's story on
> hand, I read three different versions to the kids. I emphasized what is

a legend? What is an oral tradition? And how do stories get written down in so many ways?

Then because it seemed a good idea and the ability to synthesize many perspectives is valuable, I asked kids to write down their version of this famous legend. I was interested in how they heard it, how they changed it and how they made it their own. It seemed like a good way to figure out kids' facility with language, but I didn't have any grand plan. Or even a small one.

One child wanted to write the story down on the word processor and she composed and revised over and over until she got her story to sound and look like she wanted. Others were interested in this typed version and so I typed up their written stories. We spent so much time on this activity, I chose to put them in everyone's portfolio. Had we done a lot more of this kind of summarizing, kids would have had more choices of writing pieces to include—they wouldn't have all been the same.

For some reason, I still don't know exactly what for, but I am thinking about it, I noticed how long it took kids to write the story down. Some sat at a table for 45 minutes and wrote for 5 minutes and finished. Some finished writing the whole story in 10 minutes. I found that information interesting so I wrote it down.

Cathy's account of developing this curriculum begins with an incipient idea sparked by a colleague's comments, the serendipity of materials that fit children's interests, and her questions that put the activity in a legitimate curricular frame. She moved the activity to a deeper level when she realized that children's composing their own versions could promote skill in synthesizing. The assessment plans were vague. Cathy capitalized on a child's interest in word processing and interest spread. She made the decision to put final drafts into each portfolio. No child contested her decision—the typed, illustrated final product easily met children's standards for the kind of work they prefer to include. The final point was Cathy's informal inquiry into the time it took children to do the writing. Whatever Cathy learned, this exploration was not an exercise to check up on the children or judge how well they told the story in their own words.

These *Legend of Sleepy Hollow* pieces raise significant questions about literacy that Cathy and other teachers are eager to consider. In Bellevue, Washington, where I visited after Provincetown, teachers are developing districtwide Literacy Portfolios, including elements designed to aggregate information about children's interaction with text. They find the details of Cathy's portfolios interesting and teachers are hungry for talk about them. On both coasts teachers are asking: How do children make meaning of stories? Is one child's meaning "better" than another child's? What skills are involved in synthesizing? Can synthesizing be taught or would this attempt bring educators right back to isolating individual skills?

Portfolios that promote this inquiry make more visible what teachers really care about in their classrooms as well as what they don't yet understand. Having a collection of work and an occasion to talk provides an opening for teachers to question their practice without depending on outside assessments or curriculum experts who do not understand the local contexts of the classroom community. Portfolios in all three sites encourage this teacher-to-teacher conversation.

EXPLORING DILEMMAS AND PHILOSOPHICAL MONSTERS WITH COLLEAGUES

Cathy's learning style is quite different from the child in her class she quotes as saying: "I like to talk about ideas . . . the talking helps change my ideas . . . it doesn't really matter if the other person doesn't answer." Cathy doesn't often need to talk. Much of the time, she works out questions about practice in her head walking on the beach with her dog. She experiments in her classroom, refining her strategies for implementing her ideas, and then she offers them to colleagues. But she needs her colleagues to talk to her. In that talk they develop a common language, which contributes to her learning.

Several times during my visit, Cathy brings her quiet presence to the group. Her gentle comments at lunch or on the playground are slipped in almost unnoticed. "You know my thing. You've got to keep kids' voices" is the way she makes her positions known. But as clear as it is that Cathy teaches from her own philosophical values and contributes her own voice in collegial settings, and as clear as it is that she thinks deeply about children and education, she leaves plenty of space for colleagues' thoughts. They are exploring together.

Whose Standards?

In contrast to a portfolio, a single numerical test score measures the trivial, robs learning of its rich complexity, and reduces the possibilities for children to demonstrate their learning. Those who trust test scores say "When in doubt, quantify," but Cathy does not value the certainty of numbers when used to rate children. On the contrary, Cathy and her colleagues struggle to answer larger and more ambiguous questions. But in between the child and the seekers after certainty are some gaps to be filled.

Though she focuses intensely on each child as an individual being, and believes in the benefit of teaching children to look at themselves in relation to the standards and criteria set forth in *Dimensions,* she is not yet willing to concede the absence of a conventionally standard way to write, paint, and think. "Whose standards?"—the question so much talked about in other communities—is only faintly pressing on her in Provincetown. The tension around which standards and who sets them is not as acute as in some places. Teachers in urban schools must think through the arguments for and against standard English every time they interact with a child around writing or decide how and whether to correct speech.

The tension Cathy feels is different. Cathy is unconflicted about children's need to engage in activities that are meaningful to them. She believes deeply that educators must accept children's standards for their work and that each child has an aesthetic that must be respected. But when Cathy thinks about life beyond her classroom, she recognizes the radical nature of trying to see the world from the child's perspective and feels the pressure to think differently.

Resolving such issues is a process; in the interim the pedagogical ground is soft. Cathy recognizes that her response to children's work is centrally intertwined with the standards question. While she always accepts children's work as they offer it for portfolios, and resists the common temptation to only include a child's "best work," she acknowledges that if she lined all the *Legend of Sleepy Hollow* summaries in a row, she would find some wanting. Rather than appreciating the child's intentions and personal imprint, she would concern herself with (and maybe worry about) the children whose summaries lacked details or were incoherently organized or did not meet the *Dimensions* standard for clear communication. In a late-night phone conversation, she wistfully alludes to the reality of teaching in a public school, how she would like to be free of the pressure for reading and spelling skills. She would like to be able to see the value in a child's work as the child does and be comfortable with child's personal standard rather than what the upper school requires. But the issues are not easy and the real world intrudes from an entirely different vantage point—at an after-school meeting of the Faculty Assessment Committee.

The Philosophical Monster of Mythical Standards

At an after-school meeting of the Faculty Assessment Committee, the issue of standards comes up obliquely. The Provincetown Elementary portfolios are at the moment a way to give parents more information than a grade or a standardized test, but some parents want definite answers to this question: How is my child doing in relation to other children and in relation to grade level? Portfolios cannot provide a firm answer. To suggest one, the not-yet-adopted but much-worked-on report card tentatively specifies categories: below standard, meets standard, exceeds standard. The assumption that these "standards" are norm-referenced rankings pegged to grade levels—which is the way external standards are often understood—is not universal, but is the way parents and teachers often think about them. Parents don't see grade-level rankings as being as arbitrary as they are. Testmakers and textbook publishers contribute to this categorizing of children by reading level and the public in general is unready or unable to put forth a contrary point of view. Thus misunderstanding is rampant.

In this Faculty Assessment Committee meeting, which Cathy chairs, someone asks (rhetorically, perhaps): "If you are going to have three categories, do end-of-the-trimester standards for first grade exist somewhere? Do you have an actual written down set of standards?"

"No," says a teacher. "Philosophically, it's a monster."

The logician persists: "Then you are grading kids against mythical standards. If you say children are below standard or exceeding standards, you must have some real standards set down."

The others resist that position, though anyone buying into the reality of norm-referenced grade levels might accept it as logical. Someone else voices what this faculty already knows at a gut level: Standards pegged to a specific time frame would mean that if a first grader starts out in December below some arbitrary standard, the child will never catch up. The discomfort is palpable. While some school systems might welcome such absolutism, this faculty does not. Someone speaks for the group: "We can't have that," and people move on to another topic. This is a value-laden and humanely motivated evasion of the standards issue. The discussion does not resolve how to report rankings to parents nor does it look for an opening to educate parents to other ways of thinking about standards that do not imply rankings and are more in keeping with the teachers' values.

Judgments

Portfolios used for accountability purposes far removed from the individual child are not what Cathy has in mind. Nor are her portfolios designed to be judged. "I resist any kind of judgment in portfolios. I have report cards; I have 18 years of experience; I don't want to confuse validating kids' learning with judging them." But life is not so simple. She has seen the faculty interest in tying the report card to portfolios ("But how?" she asks). As for putting judgments on portfolios, Cathy says, "You can't judge some of the standards. You can't judge the dimensions of Attitudes and Approaches, that's just the way kids are. Some people need to talk out their learning. A quiet classroom doesn't help them. But just because I think some student's work is not meeting some criteria on the *Dimensions* list doesn't mean that child isn't a good student. It isn't so black and white; we've had to compromise. Two years ago, I used to have a visceral reaction to using portfolios for evaluation, but now I haven't decided. I know I can't think it through alone. I need my colleagues."

Provincetown does not even give report card grades from kindergarten through third grade. Within the upper grades a range of opinions exists about how much standardization of portfolios is possible, even tolerable. But no one would ever consider grading a portfolio. Discussions about grading—possibly threatening as teachers share their most deeply held values about their classrooms—often involve compromise and negotiation. Cathy recognizes that her classroom does sometimes pose a problem for some upper-grade teachers who think the lower school is "loosey goosey" and that children are missing something in the early childhood wing because teachers don't teach a heavy dose of basic skills. But, and Cathy repeats, with emphatic relief, "*no one* at my school would ever consider grading a portfolio."

Opposition

The work with Project Zero on portfolios brought some opposition. During 1991–1992, the second year of their work together, rare political trouble surfaced in the form of *one* complaining parent. "Why is Harvard using my child as a guinea pig?" he wanted to know. The superintendent invited Project Zero to hold open community forums, and the small furor subsided. To an outsider, this event was not a furor, but Cathy's vivid memories of this incident still rankle her, which is a reminder of how minimal dissent in a small town sends wide ripples and what can happen when schools don't communicate enough with parents.

Perhaps nothing could have assuaged that disgruntled parent and he moved shortly to another town, but communicating with parents is still a major topic on Provincetown's agenda. In this small community much of the communication is in passing—parents and teachers live side by side, shop at the same stores, and go to the same movies. The school laments that they have not always made a formal effort to communicate their assessment policies to parents. When individual parents complain about the absence of uniform standards and class rankings, teachers feel the sting. This year, they promise themselves, they will do a better job.

Finding Time to Reflect

Once teachers connect with what portfolios can teach them about children, the shortage of time for that learning nags at them. The Provincetown faculty uses an assessment technique called the Collaborative Assessment Conference developed by researchers at Project Zero, which allows for a collaborative, descriptive, and evaluative review of children's work in a highly structured setting. In particular, the faculty uses the CAC in conjunction with the Building-Based-Support Team, which oversees referrals to special education. Teachers, including Cathy, bring portfolios to this committee in order to look at children's work with colleagues when they consider extraordinary interventions. But it is hard to find enough regular time to share and reflect on students who do well or don't present serious problems. Cathy regrets the lack of time for looking together at children's work. "We do have a place to bring kids and their portfolios when we have questions about a child. But there is never enough time. Never." Still, the PVMES faculty have enviable opportunities for collaboration and growth, and description of children and work is not the only valuable talk. For 15 years, this faculty has been meeting after school in committees to govern the school.

Transmitting the Culture: New Teachers and Portfolios

An important arena for ongoing collegial deliberation is the Faculty Assessment Committee, whose responsibility is to consider issues around portfolios and report cards. This is the same committee that raised the standards issue. I am present for the first meeting of the 1993 school year, which convenes in the sunny, commodious library. Rather than sitting in the bean-bag chairs chosen earlier in the day by the children, seven adults sit around a nearby conference table.

Today before the meeting officially begins, Cathy recounts a question she was asked by a teacher at the last workshop she gave for a nearby school system : "Do you have blocks in your classroom?"

"Yes, of course."

"Well, then, how do they work?"

"Children build with them," Cathy says, marveling at the oddity of the question, even in the retelling.

"No, not building blocks. Time blocks, you know, double periods."

That the teacher did not understand the uninterrupted time supporting this faculty's long-developed practice brings a smile to the group.

I am surprised that this group takes the blocks in the second grade so much for granted. Too many second graders sit at desks day after day filling in workbooks, waiting for their turn to join a reading group whose level is predetermined by a pencil-and-paper test—until the teacher asks them to switch to math workbooks. Children do not build with blocks in these classrooms.

The task of today's meeting is to step back and look at their school's progress by comparing their reform efforts with Beverly Anderson's chart in the September 1993 issue of *Educational Leadership*. The acting principal has asked them to look at this chart, "The Continuum of Systemic Change," to identify gaps for future work. They tick off what they have already achieved: time arranged to support flexible instruction, everything to do with networks (Project Zero and Four Seasons), active learning, alternative assessments. Time to reflect together? They agree that lack of time to talk is a gap, and so is communication with parents, which leads them to discuss the philosophical monster of mythical standards.

Another thread running through the meeting drives home a question to the whole teaching profession: How can a group that has shared responsibility for rich portfolio work bring a new teacher into their culture?

Listening to all this heady school reform talk would have daunted me as a first-year teacher, since my most pressing need was keeping children in some semblance of order for public lunch line-up. Provincetown's new teacher is much more experienced, but she has never "done portfolios." She apologizes for her many queries as she returns to portfolios throughout the agenda. Responding to her genuine desire to figure out their local practice, the faculty offers impromptu recommendations suffused with a reassuring welcome: "We've been looking at this portfolio work so long, it is great to have new eyes." Their good advice, generated by a colleague's urgent need to know and passed on from teacher to teacher, may help reduce gaps between any senior teacher's "Remember, we've been doing it for years" and recent arrival's "So what's a new person to do?" These recommendations, out in the open, in teachers' own language, convey in my notes what they believe to be essentials. These intuitions guide new teachers' learning and pass the culture along:

1. You don't have to produce portfolios all at once. Portfolios are a process.
2. You can't *ever* do everything.
3. Don't treat portfolios as an add-on; integrate each piece with your teaching as you gain experience.
4. Don't kill yourself with overworry or kids will hate it.
5. If a child asks specifically for work from gym or art or music, encourage it but you don't have to collect it for all kids or all specialists.
6. Don't decide in advance how long kids will take to pull pieces for their portfolio and reflect on them. Be flexible. This is valuable learning time.

7. Don't pull pieces too often or kids get bored. Biweekly or even monthly works.
8. Relax. We've had years of reflection time. We'll help you.
9. Ask the kids. They'll tell you.

"We'll help you" and "Ask the kids"—these twin prongs, genuine collegiality and teaching/learning so internalized by children that teachers can learn from their students, contribute to everyone's growth. That's what school reform is for. Portfolios only connect.

New Work/New Dilemma: Must Portfolios Be Standardized?

In the summer of 1993, three faculty members, including Jane Rowe and Four Seasons Team members Kris Eastman (now moved away) and Helen Motto, wrote a report on how portfolios could/should be used in the future. This report will come up for discussion before the Faculty Assessment Committee that Cathy chairs. A substantial piece of work, it is entitled "The Summer Portfolio Project: Using the Collaborative Assessment Method to Assess Program Effectiveness in Meeting Needs of Students in the Mainstream."

This report represents the first formal attempt to think through the use of portfolios beyond individual classrooms. Do these portfolios, so central to collegial conversation and to teachers', students', and parents' own understanding, have any use beyond those already important purposes? The question raises two related troublesome new dilemmas: (1) Can or should portfolios be used for program assessment ? (2) Can or should portfolios be standardized?

Using the Project Zero methods for looking at the portfolios, this committee considered 20 fifth- and sixth-grade portfolios to ascertain whether the school was adequately serving special-needs children in regular classrooms. The committee found that as they are, portfolios lack information about the context of children's work and therefore do not yield enough evidence to judge. The committee sensibly asked: Do we know if "included" students actually are participating if we don't know how they completed their work? The report concluded:

> In order to address the effectiveness of a program for any student, it is necessary to understand how a given task is completed, and with what degree of assistance. It may also be helpful to know the nature of the assignment, and indeed, whether it was an assignment or an activity initiated by the student.

The report writers felt strongly that these "missing voices" in the portfolios caused "problems in reading" them. This means that no teacher or student explanations exist in the portfolio to answer questions asked by various portfolio readers. Solving the problem of missing voices will necessitate rethinking what accompanies each student- or faculty-selected portfolio piece. Faculty will have to decide when "apparatus" (my word for everything in a portfolio beyond the work itself) is a valuable contribution to the student record and when it overshadows the work itself. Management issues follow. If providing context becomes too big a job, will it be easier to leave a significant piece out rather than provide a written context for it? The collections of work, the committee also says, are "too highly individualized to determine whether a program meets the needs of a wide range of students." Therefore, if portfolios are to be used for accountability, they will have to be more standardized.

In a move to use the portfolios for accountability, the committee calls for a "standardization of evidence" and says: "Portfolios can provide the documentation to support teacher observations about the effectiveness of specific curriculum for enhanced inclusion IF a standard structure to portfolios is formulated. Given a standard structure, there is accountability." It is, they say, "commonalties that provide a structure for viewing a student's individual growth as well as for comparing progress among students." The committee recommends that specific items be placed in the portfolio within loose time frames and that "the 'teacher's voice' should be evident in any sample submitted."

This sharpening of the portfolios might well produce another round of thinking that informs teaching. But it also raises questions that trouble thoughtful practitioners. Must you standardize portfolios? Does standardization blind teachers to children's strengths? Do commonalties take away from their expressiveness and the way they make meaning of their world? What is gained by standardization? A Provincetown faculty member asks, "Does using portfolios for accountability take their 'freshness' away?"

This report is now before the Faculty Assessment Committee, which Cathy chairs. Cathy does not know the answers to these questions, but she knows from past experience that the power of thinking them through with colleagues will yield a clearer picture of the issues and a chance to sort out what is not yet understood. Confronting these matters is uncharted territory for the Provincetown faculty.

THE GROWTH OF TEACHER LEADERSHIP

Cathy does not hesitate to delineate how her thinking has developed along with the portfolios over the last four years. She has changed, not only in her relationship to children, but in her relationship to their work. She knows children take what they do more seriously in the face of her deep interest, especially when she writes down their thoughts about their work. She thinks portfolios have made her more systematic; she no longer collects work randomly just to send home at the end of the year. She now knows more about each child's process from their work receipts, their portfolio visits (when they look carefully at the work they have collected), and the reflective pieces they write. She has improved her ability to develop clear, accurate questions to ask of children about both their work and their process. She feels more accountable, since she has evidence at her fingertips from a child's portfolio to report to parents or make a case to the Building-Based Support Team. And, she says, "I now have real respect for what is personal about kid's work. I can see that children own their learning."

Cathy has developed and elaborated a particular kind of portfolio: an ongoing collection of work, carefully chosen by both teacher and child to document growth over time and provide a portrait of that child. She has mastered the management of the time and the storage requirements. She has integrated strategies for children's self-reflection into the curricular and classroom structures as naturally as she builds community. She provides varied and compelling experiences for children based on multiple intelligences within the Provincetown curriculum. She makes use of her knowledge of the learning process with children. She contends with the ambiguities and large questions that arise from portfolios as they have developed at her school.

These accomplishments did not happen overnight or in a vacuum. Cathy acknowledges that without colleagues, administrative support, networks, and academic collaborators, she might be isolated in her classroom, repeating each year what she did before. She values the administrative support in the form of paid summer time for collegial committee work, meetings held within the school day, and a stimulating relationship with respectful university researchers. Her participation in the Four Seasons Project reaffirms her place in the national dialogue and gives her a network for support; she is not alone in figuring out the tough dilemmas. Exposure to the concept of multiple intelligences through Project Zero has made Cathy more aware of the complicated nature of learning and deepened her conception of the myriad ways children learn. Without these opportunities for growth, she might have actually left teaching, as she almost did before her leave of absence. Instead she has become a leader in and beyond her school.

As teachers, in collaboration with networks and their own colleagues, begin to articulate and resolve the dilemmas of public accountability, their questions become sharper. When teachers have the opportunity to untangle these questions, and figure out ever-more rigorous processes and strategies for assessment, possibilities open up for new understandings about teaching and learning. Teachers who articulate their practice have more control over the way it evolves. Teachers who face the hard issues beyond their own classrooms are more prepared to enter discussions of policy and to raise their voices in developing organizational structures that support their work. When teachers engage in these processes and increase their knowledge, they build their capacity to create more possibilities to enhance children's learning.

Teachers' knowledge grows from participating in talk beyond their classrooms; others outside the classroom benefit from teachers' knowledge of child development and daily classroom life. This experience in articulating practice readies them to have a voice at the policy table. Without that articulated understanding, their knowledge remains unspoken and local (not just in the realm of policy, but in research arenas as well). When teachers join policy discussions, their knowledge adds to policymakers' more distant perspective. Teachers' practice improves as a result of the bigger frame, and policymakers gain a closer view of the classroom. Were policymakers actually to go into the classroom with teachers as interpretive guides and teachers to take on policymaking positions for a time, that would deepen the cyclical benefits.

But teacher leadership creates an unintended consequence and causes new pressures. Becoming a leader outside the classroom gives teachers opportunities to get better at thinking and talking about practice. This means not only that become even more thoughtful teachers, but also that their presence is in more demand by outside groups, thus increasing pressure to choose between the classroom and the conference table or the speaker's podium. Integrating these professional responsibilities into teachers' school lives is possible, but is not easy and happens only rarely.

When teachers are seen as either less than competent professionals or as time-serving functionaries who are not fully invested in their jobs, it is natural for parents, school boards, and political leaders to call for rigid standards for judging children and teachers alike. In this diminished view of the teaching force, trusting teachers endangers children—since it allows teachers to exercise judgment beyond their abilities or slacken their efforts in the classroom. But if teachers are encouraged to build their own capacity as they are in Provincetown, the scenario changes. Cathy is not unique. As teachers are supported with time, collaborative colleagues, and authority over their own practice, they become increasingly trustworthy to conduct their own assessments. Perhaps as trustworthiness increases, demands for mechanical accountability to distant stakeholders and assessment instruments will decrease. Perhaps teachers themselves will be trusted to answer questions about their own effectiveness.

Ideally, accountability requires that schools and the people in them create responsible and responsive practices that improve teaching (Darling-

Hammond, 1993). In their continuing and cumulative portfolio work, Cathy and the Provincetown Elementary faculty have created processes that hold them accountable. As teachers increasingly become more secure about their assessments and more articulate, their approach looks more systematic, credible, and communicable, less capricious and more rigorous. Considering Cathy's process, along with her portfolios, should help outsiders to assess the care and consistency of thought that has gone into her work and convince them that she has a repertoire of appropriate strategies for teaching diverse children and that she has ability to judge their strengths and weaknesses. One might ask—and policymakers often do—what difference portfolios make for children's learning. How much better are children reading, writing, and thinking as a result of portfolios? If only a quantifiable measure of children's learning will satisfy the questioner, the answer will remain as murky as ever. The measurement question does not weigh heavily on Cathy in her classroom, where she and the children are actively engaged in making meaning of their world.

But for that time to arrive where Cathy and her colleagues are trusted, the classroom has to become more permeable to outsiders. Policymakers and others must come closer to the classroom. Cathy's portfolio work—in the classroom, in folders, and in conversation—is open to local scrutiny and ready to be seen and discussed by students, parents, administrators, policymakers, and the Provincetown public. They should look.

CHAPTER 2

Portfolios in Bellevue

Opportunity for Inquiry and Mandate for Measurement

I love our portfolio process, but I love it because when Johnny and his mom and I all sit together we find joy in what he has accomplished, that it is "good enough" because he has made progress. Frankly, I don't care how other children score compared to Johnny.

Barb Renfrow-Baker

I don't know how I feel about scoring; I need to play with it more. Our group got high reliability, but it doesn't help me to know a kid is a 3 on a rubric of 1–5. If it tells the district how kids are doing in reading and reduces the reliance on test scores, I will support standardizing some things in the short term to get people to see the value of portfolios.

I keep a lot of what I know about children and their work in my head. Descriptive Review gave me a way to discuss and share my observations. I now go through those categories (physical presence, emotional tenor, relationships, academics, interests) while I'm in the shower. I think about kids who have slipped away, who I have big questions about, who are struggling. I use the categories and try to figure out what to do. Then I make time for those children in my day. Thinking about kids like this is a habit now.

Marla English

Though children on both coasts startle me with the same question—"You live in New York City. Have you been to FAO Schwartz?"—traveling from an easternmost Atlantic shore to the Pacific Northwest is a major shift of climate, culture, and scale. At the Woodridge Elementary School in foggy Bellevue, Washington, Richard Scarry's *Book of Transportation* in Japanese is a choice at reading time. Four hundred children eat *nachos* (the fat content label undoubtedly rendered inaccurate by the fifth-grade helpers who determine the portions) or trade sushi and peanut butter from their lunch boxes. A table of English-speaking children finds it unremarkable that Kimoko is composing a piece entitled in their language "My Dog," but horizontally filling up page after page with *kanji* in the contemporary Japanese fashion.

On the playground Noah rushes up to Suki, interrupting her story-writing, with a request to make him an origami envelope. She quickly and precisely folds Noah's proffered notebook paper into an envelope, smoothing the creases with her flattened pencil. Reading his disappointed face as he sees it will not keep safe the tiny pieces of paper he's holding in his hand, she says (with some asperity), "You know, origami is for decoration, not for use." As he studies the paper, no longer an envelope, he responds to her lesson with feeling: "I really love these folds."

This incidental but essential teaching and learning happen naturally here amid a student body that is 64% Anglo, 22% Asian; 8% Latino, 4% African-American, and 2% Native-American. *Here* is suburban Bellevue, a 60-minute drive in rush hour from Seattle Center, where Suki and Kimoko and Noah are among 44 students in a first- through third-grade classroom. The class is taught by team teachers Marla English and Barb Renfrow-Baker, who joined Four Seasons through their connection with the Foxfire Teacher Outreach Network and became National Faculty members during the summer of 1993.

Bellevue is the fourth largest city in Washington, and is, I am told by an envious mother from a nearby town, "the Lincoln-Continental of Washington State, where the parents make up any money the schools don't provide." That description might be true at the "Gold Coast" schools where upscale means living close to the water, but not at the Woodridge School in central Bellevue. This school sits at the top of a hill lined with modest ranch houses and serves the Bellevue School District's largest catchment area. Though reports occasionally circulate of parents who complain about "those children," over the last 10 years the Woodridge School has taken pleasure in becoming the educational home to an increasing number of newly arrived immigrant families. Approximately 70 out of 400 children at Woodridge receive free or reduced-price lunch (proportionally half as many as Provincetown), but only one data entry clerk knows who they are, since every child "buys" lunch with the same computer card. Some new families at the Woodridge School own houses and work as computer experts at the nearby Microsoft corporate headquarters. Others live in small rental apartments with large extended families and pick seasonal crops. Unlike Provincetown Elementary, transiency challenges the teachers: Only 25% of children starting kindergarten are the same children who finish fifth grade. Woodridge is among the most economically and culturally diverse schools in Bellevue, but at least at the elementary level, the growing diversity is so unremarkable that I have to probe for this demographic information about the school community.

Depending on your stance, the Bellevue School District budget is either ample or modest; surrounding districts have both more and less money. Up-to-date new equipment is paid for by the city's recently passed technology bond issue, which means there is a fax in the teachers' room and next door a high-quality desktop publishing center. Teachers take home computers on loan, have VCRs in their classrooms, and camcorders, if they want. But a lack of school buses requires a complicated shuffle that dislocates families and teachers alike. Teachers govern their schools locally, which is an advance in school reform terms, but consequently the central administration is pared down to a cost-saving, sometimes stress-producing minimum.

The Bellevue District encourages individual schools to allocate their own resources. The Woodridge principal divides the school budget money for supplies equally among all the classrooms, and requires each classroom to support its own laminating, xeroxing, photo developing, and book binding. In order to lower class size, Woodridge exists without a full-time librarian or a reading specialist. Just as schools make choices, teachers also choose among options. Teachers can spend their allocated money on field trips, visiting experts, or even their own in-service education. As teachers do everywhere, they often choose to spend their own money for trade books and other basic supplies. Bellevue inclines toward choices on all levels—from the district to the classroom—and the long history of giving teachers choices predictably influences how they go about making assessment policy.

In 1990, the Bellevue School Board charged the district with finding alternatives to standardized testing. Unlike the schoolwide initiative at Fenway or in Provincetown, this district-inspired directive required any solution to include measures of comparability, reliability, and validity. The district recognized the complexity of this challenge and wisely set a five-year goal for development. As always, Bellevue involved teachers in choosing how to proceed. Four districtwide volunteer study groups met for a year and all pointed to portfolios as the best solution. Now, in its third year, teachers in the Bellevue Literacy Assessment Project are helping their schools pilot this new approach to student assessment, all the while debating the tradeoffs between the district-required standardized portfolios that follow testing technology norms of validity and reliability and more individualized portfolios that reflect the children they see in their own classrooms. I have come to document what these dual purpose portfolios look like through teachers' eyes.

HARMONY AND DISSONANCE:
THE CHORDS OF CLASSROOM PRACTICE

It is still pitch dark at 6:45 A.M. when Marla English and Barb Renfrow-Baker arrive at school for an appointment with a student teacher. It is equally dark when they leave at 8:30 P.M., after a parent/faculty standing committee meeting on assessment.

Today Marla English wears an intensely blue and orange angora-trim sweater with a Halloween theme, a present on her recent birthday. The birthday flowers her husband sent are on the table she demarcates as her work space. With 12-hour days their norm (they never take work home or talk on the phone), Marla and Barb have made their classroom into a comfortable place to pursue their professional careers. With word processors, modem, microwave, refrigerator, an impressive professional library, their own files, and an ample stash of food, they offer a welcoming center to children, student teachers, parent and community volunteers, and colleagues from their own faculty. It is here that they do the thinking and writing that prepares them for the wider professional world. Marla has recently returned from a New Standards Language Arts meeting in Boston, Barb from attending the Northwest Mathematics Conference in Portland. They both savor the collaborative classroom they share, confirming what we know: that good schools for children are good places for adults.

Shared Classroom/Shared Learning

Marla and Barb work together in practiced harmony in and out of their classroom. At the open evening assessment meeting they accomplish their preplanned goals in sync with each other. The agenda is tricky and a small handful of parents threatens to derail the meeting by talking out of turn, whispering to each other, and confining their contributions to their own children rather than the larger central assessment issues. On this night they want more spelling tests, no health education that takes away from "valuable learning time," and a forum for their complaint that "no one ever listens to our perspectives, even though we have been consistently attending this committee and saying the same thing for years." They are a decided minority of 4 in the larger group of 30, and others are respectful, but apparently there has been a growing feeling that meetings are not as professional as they could be and the meetings are not moving ahead. Marla and Barb in tandem with Rob Brown, another Four Seasons member, gently urge the group to list their expectations for participation. Marla, co-chairing with a parent, and Barb, managing the magic marker and the chart paper, move the group through an exercise that results in the adoption of written guidelines for meeting behavior. These include basics such as starting and ending on time and also more subtle agreements that get at the group's tone: "Say what you want in the meeting, not after the meeting." At 8:30 P.M., when the meeting breaks up, Barb and Marla are still talking about the meeting with the same kind of animation they began with more than 12 hours ago.

They thrive on their talk together. When I asked to visit her classroom in order to document the pioneering portfolio practice in Bellevue that I have heard about for years, Marla said, "We are like one." Marla and Barb are in their second year of team teaching together. It is true that they are working toward the same purposes in their classroom, but they each bring separate skills to their teaching, differing philosophical nuances to their discussions, and unique chemistry to their relationships with children. Almost imperceptibly they signal their thoughts about classroom routines to be managed, clerical jobs to be done, and children or parents to be nurtured. Who manages the classroom transitions is a matter of eye contact and where they are standing more than an advance plan. Their pooled strengths enrich their teaching and provide evidence of how collaborative classrooms can benefit both teachers and their students.

After a year at Sarah Lawrence College, a degree from the University of Washington in anthropology, and six years as a corporate executive assistant, Barb returned to graduate school to follow the career path of her mother and her aunts, who are all teachers. Barb did her student teaching in Marla's class and then had a self-contained first and second grade under Marla's mentoring. The next year, they chose to work together. Barb is now happily in her third year of teaching and knows how fortunate she is to be learning in the company of Marla. In her first year the principal also made Barb the Woodridge School Math Leader, an unusual show of confidence in a new teacher. She is strong in mathematics, and her imprint on the classroom shows in the collections of carefully graphed data displayed prominently on the walls and her interactions with children around big mathematical ideas.

Marla is the veteran. With a psychology degree from Temple University specializing in Test Administration and Construction and master's degrees in both Special Education and Educational Administration, Marla has been teaching students of all ages from early childhood through high school for over 26 years, the last 8 of them at Woodridge. For 2 years, she taught the profoundly handicapped class and it is a Woodridge legend how she is forever indebted to the only faculty member willing to share a wing when she had a child who screamed all day. After 2 years, she initiated Woodridge's first team-taught multiage group, now in its fifth year.

Despite the imbalance in their experience, Marla trusts Barb's values and judgment. Barb values learning under Marla's tutelage. Their team relationship goes way beyond getting through the day effectively and smoothly; the conversations they have together fuel their teaching. Marla says: "As soon as I read an article, I can't wait to discuss it so I know what I think." These days, Barb is her first audience. Marla holds a lot of information about children and teaching in her head and by her own admission conversations with Barb allow her to say out loud what she knows. "I am an interpersonal intelligence," she says, referring to one of the multiple intelligences Howard Gardner (1991) postulates. Barb is particularly good—even gifted—at the collegial talk that goes along with teaming, perhaps a result of constant conversation with her mother, who had a long career as a "leading teacher" in a nearby district. Barb and Marla often take early morning walks together so they can talk about teaching and children. "Never personal stuff," Barb assures me, as if I might have missed that what they love talking about is children, learning, and teaching.

A shared classroom is an extraordinary opportunity to refine the craft of teaching. Just as children make meaning of their world at home and at school, teachers reach for an understanding of what happens in their own classrooms. Not just some special teachers, but all teachers have deep but often unarticulated knowledge about their teaching. Teachers are not born with this knowledge; they hone it over years of experience as they make decisions, resolve dilemmas, and set goals in their classrooms. But when teachers are isolated, without any forums for the talk that Marla and Barb find so valuable, they lose the chance, as Cathy Skowron (1992, p. 38) says, "to put language to practice." Just as self-reflection and talk about the process of learning give children power over their own school life, so, too, teachers gain control over their always-evolving practice when they can talk about teaching and learning with others. In a good team-teaching relationship, teachers can carve out a daily place to put language to practice. That ability to step back, to hash over, to reflect, to become increasingly clear about the dilemmas and decisions that underlie their pedagogy, is how craft develops. The Oxford English Dictionary's first definition of craft is the art, skill, and intellectual power over a medium. Developing the craft of teaching through talk is an honorable challenge.[1]

Sometimes a Foxfire Classroom

Marla and Barb represent Foxfire in the Four Seasons Project. Foxfire looks to single teachers, and promotes school reform through changed classroom practice, classroom by classroom. Refined over the past 26 years, the Foxfire approach echoes the philosophy of John Dewey and is characterized by democratic involvement of the students in governing their classes. Students create work from their own experience and interests and together students and teachers develop a two-way link to academic goals. Foxfire classrooms vary, but most observers would agree that Marla runs "a Foxfire classroom," even if she sees the roots of her practice elsewhere.

Today, as Marla talks about the evolution of her practice, she is especially mindful of how much her father—recently hospitalized and terminally ill—contributed to her classroom vision, long before she joined Foxfire. She reminisces nostalgically:

> This classroom has elements of my childhood. I lived all over the
> United States and outdoors was my play world. I built things; I wrote
> plays. We lived in a trailer. My father was a construction project
> manager for a corporation that moved him all over. I was in 8 to 9
> schools every year. The crew that worked for my Dad was my commu-
> nity. Since we had no room for toys inside, Dad brought us industrial
> discards like spools to play with outside. We played in the creek. My
> classroom is like my childhood environment, though my childhood
> play was always outside of school.
>
> During my elementary years, I gravitated to drama and I loved
> books, but I got bled upon in writing, by which I mean I couldn't
> write, wasn't asked to write, and most writing I did was copying. It
> was my own blood—I got wounded about my inadequacies in writing.
> I don't remember writing stories, so plays were my stories. I was into
> managing large groups so I didn't have to write things down; I just
> had to assign kids parts.

From observing her in the classroom, it is easy to imagine a young Marla organizing playground dramatics in a new school each month; her take-charge but subtle leadership permeates. "So are we going to finish those portfolio entry slips this morning or this afternoon?" is her way of reminding someone else to do the job. By her own admission, Marla thrives on children who have ideas that never occurred to her and problems that she has no idea how to solve. She says she has always trusted children to take from the environment what they need and balanced that trust with careful attention to instructing them in what she thinks they need. Marla fills her classroom with opportunities for children to invent their own projects, dramas, constructions, and writings. Whatever the origins of her teaching, her practice fits within "The Foxfire Approach: Perspectives and Core Practices" (Appendix A).

Networking is central to Foxfire. The Foxfire Outreach Network develops state and local connections among teachers. Typically, newcomers take a Level 1 course, as it is called, which provides an intense 30–40-hour graduate course or staff-development program and engages teachers in the Foxfire process—both the experience and reflection on it. Foxfire follow-up support can include meetings, classroom visits by other teachers or coordinators, conferences, newsletters, teleconferences, *Hands-On* (a national journal written by and for teachers), and more specialized courses.

In a story characteristic of Foxfire's teacher-to-teacher approach, Barb describes on-line[2] how she and Marla came to join Foxfire, and then Four Seasons:

> In fall of 1991, Lynn Beebe scheduled a meeting in Bellevue and came with the Foxfire/Soundfire Coordinator to advertise Foxfire. The meeting happened to be at our school, so Rob Brown, Carolyn Kradjan, Marla and I went. We got excited and took the level 1 training from Gayle McKnight in August, 1992. Before we actually enrolled, I'd logged onto the Soundfire computer network to snoop around and saw this name from my past—Carol Coe. I mean we're talking *past*. She was my debate coach in high school. So I sent her a message and she encouraged our attendance at the Level 1 course. In the fall we attended the Soundfire network meetings, which were held almost monthly that year. Then in January 1993, at a Soundfire meeting Linda Quinn and Carol Coe told us about Four Seasons and handed us the application. We eagerly sent off a letter and the four of us plus Lynn Beebe became a Foxfire Four Seasons team. (Dec. 13, 1993).

Over two days with Marla and Barb, I see how their print- and materials-rich environment supports individual initiative and galvanizes children to solve real-life problems in a setting stimulating enough to keep children interested, even in their third year in the same classroom. Though it is often hard to tease out influences on practice over as many years as Marla and Barb have accumulated, their constant conversation puts them in touch with how their recent experience with Foxfire has sharpened their practice. They describe how they have newly balanced the individual and the group, tapping the children's own interests and teaching the processes that make for a democratic classroom. Marla says, "I know I am there when I say not 'my classroom' but 'our classroom.'" Barb elaborates: "After we took the Foxfire course, we put more decisions in the children's hands. When the block building area grew so big that it infringed on the class meeting area, we put the problem to the children. Kids generated options, and finally came up with a so-so solution, but even though we were skeptical, we let it stick.

And it works. Children also make decisions all the way from how to handle missing recess equipment to what to study for social studies."

Referring to the explicit Foxfire notion that what is taught should be useful in the world outside of school, Marla adds: "I began to notice more carefully where in life children use the skills I teach." She adds, "My classroom is more like the world. People in life are not isolated in groups with their same age birthmates." Here she lays out the basis for her thinking about real-world connections to her classroom:

> Teacher-driven curriculum is not useful. If I invent the curriculum without kids it will be fragmented and without meaning in their lives. Though such curriculum may prove that I am clever at teaching my agenda, it is useless to kids. If I can't make sure kids understand the real world connections to an activity, and if I can't put the decision-making in their hands, then I ask myself whether I should be doing that activity.
>
> I now provide math activities that involve purchasing real things for the classroom. I say to kids, "You think about what math materials we need to do a better job of math. Look through the catalogue to see what we need." Getting kids to decide what we need to do more of in math is the important real life skill. It is another lifelong skill to set goals, to observe our own work and make decisions about where we want to go with it. I want kids to express themselves in writing without me telling them what to write. Other domains matter, too. If mom's drinking is the real world for a kid, I ask myself what am I doing to help that child have survival skills so when she leaves school she can cope.

Foxfire does not focus directly on assessment, but in an on-line conversation, Barb explicates her understanding of what assessment means to her from the Foxfire perspective:

> I'm trying to boil and bubble this down into the gooey essence of it all. For me, with my current experience, Foxfire means helping individual students develop their own problems, their own assessments, and their own rubrics. I think the essence of Foxfire assessment as I have woven it into my teaching is that students set their own standards and take responsibility for reaching them.

Connections with the wider community matter in Foxfire. Every year kids in this class share what they've learned in an annual event to which children invite parents, grandparents, children who were in this class from years past, and former student teachers. After a potluck dinner and a performance (usually from the social studies curriculum), the audience goes home and the class sleeps over in the school gym. The principal makes pancakes for breakfast.

Time and Space in a Complex Classroom

Before the children arrive, Marla oversees the minutiae that ensure that the classroom philosophy stays live. She advises a student teacher on whom to invite to do pumpkin math with small groups of children ("Fathers, make sure you invite fathers; we always have moms"); instructs student teachers on the size of brads needed for a display and the correct way to fill out district forms, rules on a date for a committee meeting ("Two parents can't do it on Hanukkah, so change it."); checks that two portfolios are ready to take to the district portfolio meeting the next day; and asks rhetorically: "Should we close the block area today because we have the Australian mini-floats for the Walkathon there and space is crunched?" Barb works at the computer, retrieving and sending the daily on-line messages that serve as Woodridge's communication, sparing her partner this task.

When all 44 children arrive in this multiage first- to third-grade classroom, time is measured without reference to the clock; things happen "before snack" and "after second recess." Since Bellevue does not have enough buses, the district staggers arrival and dismissal times. Classes start for Woodridge, "a late start school," at 9:30 A.M. Teachers are not the only ones who arrive early; some children have been here since 7:00 A.M. in a day care center that charges sliding-scale fees.

Thirty children and Marla and Barb are Anglo; 11 children are of Asian descent; 3 children are Latino (and will be joined within the month by 2 more Latinos who speak only Spanish). Two children are mainstreamed, or—in the newer terminology—included with the class in spite of their motor and learning difficulties. The school has no gifted program in order to avoid fostering an elite corps of children. Certain students have English as a Second Language (ESL), Chapter 1, and special education help in the classroom. There are no pullouts here. Rather, this is a "push-in" initiative, which is the new term for an effort not to fragment children's time, relationships, and learning by removing them from the classroom at schedule-driven intervals. Marla prefers her school's terminology—"in-classroom support."

Within tight constraints of time and space, children read, write, do math, think, and perform in the company of their peers and various adults. Children sit in assigned seats that change frequently, so they have secure but rotating work and friendship groups. They arrive over a 10-minute period and go right to their tables. Forty-four children hang their coats on their chairs and put their lunch boxes, if they have them, underneath the chairs. The architects of this modern school did not install cubbies, and the district-provided rolling racks are now prohibited by the upgraded earthquake codes. Children take pencils and spiral notebooks out of large plastic boxes in front of them, put the boxes on the floor, write a simple plan for "Choice," have it checked by an adult, and by 9:40 they are all at their self-chosen work. I am astonished at the gracefulness of this multistep event accomplished without incident in these small spaces. Marla attributes the children's skill to careful training in September. Her background in educating profoundly retarded children makes her acutely aware of how to structure spaces and tasks when the environment demands it.

Marla could arrange the spaces differently; the classroom is huge, but in a scheme worked out over the years, she has chosen to leave large areas free for whole-class meetings, art, construction, block building, drama, and myriad tiny private spaces, especially useful for children to read with the many adults who appear at reading time. The children, clustered with all their paraphernalia at the tables in the center of the room, are indeed in close proximity to each other, but the classroom culture makes room for individual idiosyncrasies. Suki has added a permanent mailbox to her desk and keeps a large carton of random possessions under the table; neither teachers nor peers object when her property spills out into more public spaces. Limited space does not prevent children from engaging in large-scale projects. Peter and Howard have built a spaceship too bulky to take home on the bus, and the orange crate–sized object sits in the construction area while they think how to solve this problem.

Consistent with Foxfire "Core Practices," children's decision making is central to this classroom, and work during this period flows from their interests. The first hour of the day is devoted to work of their own choice. Children work industriously, interrupted only by an unannounced fire drill, a six-minute round trip possible only because every classroom opens to the outside. Three children are with a student teacher who is conducting a math lesson on ordinal and cardinal numbers in preparation for the whole-group lesson she will teach for her supervisor. Otherwise, children are totally in charge of what they do—within certain parameters. They are encouraged to hold to their original choices, which they record in their plan books. If they choose to play with the animals, they are required to write or draw something about their experience.

Tomoko gives me a tour of this busy classroom, pointing out all the group math work: graphs of birthdays, lost teeth, and other items of interest to 6-, 7-, and 8-year-olds. Luisa records patterns in her math book with construction paper replicas of the pattern blocks. In answer to my question as to where all these tiny paper shapes come from, Tomoko points to a shelf full of bags of them and tells me that two years ago Ms. English sent home sheets for every parent to cut out.

In the construction area several boys (yes, just boys) have arrayed rows of big nails on squares of corrugated cardboard and are attaching them to elaborate constructions built from a dismantled computer. Peter cheerfully tells me about the nails: "We're making torture zones for our spaceships." In the nearby art area three girls (yes, just girls) decorate cardboard houses with shiny red mylar fringe. Though the girls do not adapt the boys' torture zones, the boys use the red mylar fringe from the art area to decorate their spaceships, which makes them much less fierce. (At the end of the day I am touched by the sight of several boys carrying home their colorfully decorated spaceships with torture zones that look every bit as aesthetically inviting as the girls' houses.) The rest of the children work alone, with partners, and in small friendship groups. They play board games, write, draw, play with the animals, or use one of the eleven computers.

Barb alerts the children to the end of Choice with a rhythmic clapping pattern; they stop, clap it back, and quickly clean up. Richard vacuums. Within minutes, children congregate on the rug. Children are rapt as Duke (an "older," as Marla says, blurring the grade distinctions) stands before the group to share his elaborate pencil drawing. Three children are chosen to ask Duke questions (out of an eager 15 who have raised their hands). Children's questions elicit from him the following information: Duke took the whole period to draw this picture; its caption is "Be the best that you can be"; and he has drawn soldiers as well as bombs and guns in depicting the American army at war. Marienne (Vietnamese, also an "older") answers questions about the differences between Spin 50 and the Memory game she played with her friend Kiki. Josette (an "older") wrote "What I Liked About the Mice." Smiling, she reads from her paper as she clearly enunciates, "Snowball went up my arm 12 times which tickled me. I let her be in my hair. I also made a picture of patterns with colored pencils, long skinny triangles" (Barb prompts, "Scalene"). Three "olders" share today, with three different passions, three different entry points to curriculum, and three different ways of expressing it.

Then Barb takes the chair to describe the new frog tank she set up with several students. She answers questions just as the children did: How did you order the frog? Why isn't it a tadpole? And no, we don't really know the gender so I shouldn't call the frog "him."

Reading and Writing as Individuals in a Group

Snack time—10:45 on the clock—and two student teachers take charge. They devise record-keeping routines and a system to include children in serving the parent-provided pretzels and peanut butter and crackers. After snack, and a flurry of purposeful scurrying, one child from each table brings a plastic tub of books back to the table. For 20 minutes, children browse through these variously difficult high-quality trade books. How do children know which books to take? Each table devises a method. Suki, sitting among all her almost overwhelming possessions, is totally immersed in *The Boxcar Children* and doesn't even look up when Barb signals the move to "partner reading." Suddenly the room comes alive with a kaleidoscope of reading activities. "Olders" who are reading chapter books keep reading the same books, but the noise grows as children who had been sitting quietly looking through books, or reading them if they can, now join self-chosen groups to read aloud or listen. Edie turns teacher, reading to three others who sit at her feet; several pairs read oversize books with each other, and Suki keeps reading *The Boxcar Children.*

During this time, Carolyn Krajdan, Four Seasons team member who is an instructional assistant in reading and writing, joins the class to work with individuals. A retired teacher—a friend of Marla's—also appears to read with children one-on-one. That makes a total of six adults, not including me. This infusion of help means that every child has an individual turn with an adult at least once a week, documented with dated records.One-to-one reading takes place in cozy cushioned corners of the room under the aegis of teachers who know that if children are going to learn to read and to love reading they need to have uninterrupted time to read. This 50-minute reading period runs itself without adult monitoring, giving children yet another opportunity to be in charge of themselves and their learning. Again Marla attributes this self-regulation to the careful training in "literacy behavior" that she insists on at the beginning of the year. She also reminds me that only one-third of the children are new each year, making this invisible classroom management much easier. "The question I want children to have in their heads and bodies is: 'What does good reading time look like?'" Students— and teachers—at all levels might do well to have this question always in mind.

At 11:50, after more rhythmic clapping, children return to their seats. Barb announces singing and eager children retrieve their songbooks from their big plastic boxes and throw themselves into this short spurt of complicated rounds and finger play, which Barb leads effortlessly. Promptly at noon children line up for lunch.

After lunch, children play math games, then writing time follows "second recess." Out of the plastic boxes come paper and writing implements and 44 children write ongoing stories in print or in script. They compose greeting cards or picture books with magic markers, big pencils, and colored pencils, or write on the computers in Japanese, Korean, Spanish, and English. Consistent with the "push-in" rather than "pull-out" model, several adults join the class to provide special help. Now a special education aide stays by Timothy's side and the ESL teacher circulates to support children through the stages of invented spelling, or key words, or bilingual spelling lists. Some days there is an author's chair for children to share their writing, but not today. Instead Marla reads *The Kapok Tree* aloud to a rapt audience—except Josette, whose restless movements could easily be interpreted by other children as intentional poking. "Make another choice, Ms. Gifford," Marla says to her, a directive that leaves Josette in charge of her own actions.

I am struck by the realization that this is the first corrected misbehavior I have noticed all day. I flash back to an occasional unfocused child during reading, to Noah and his partner whose chess game deteriorated as they swept their pieces off the board and set it up to play "crazy chess" in their own way, complete with sound effects. I remember a minor two-child tussle on the floor away from adult eyes and some adult-ignored gum chewing. Children off course are expected to right themselves without adult intervention. The freedom from teachers whose eyes in the back of their heads catch every infraction gives children yet another chance for self-regulation. And ignoring Noah's crazy chess game gives him a chance to keep some control over his own pace when math games last an hour but his chess-playing capacity lasts only forty minutes. When teachers tolerantly ignore occasionally unfocused children, they give children a chance for some intellectual privacy and/or permission to disengage when they are out of sync with the whole group. Not all minor misbehavior is benignly neglected. Marla and Barb tell me how they must attend to Raphael's every move. Absent today, this new arrival takes their full energy as he learns the classroom culture and begins figure out when it is within the bounds to deviate from it.

Dismissed at 3:30, children gather up their constructions and books and leave. Eight children go to day care; the rest walk home, take the bus, go to other after-school program, or are picked up by parents.

The Case for a Multi-age Team-taught Classroom

Parts of this school day fit together like a tonic chord. The adult leadership, attention to detail, systematic record keeping, and ability to provide clear instruction keep the class running smoothly. Intimacy is not a word that comes to mind about the group experience; there is no daily "News" here. Yet this large-scale undertaking has other rewards. A multi-age community is built on different assumptions than those of a self-contained, single-age classroom. In this complex classroom the children span three years in age, which allows the focus to shift away from particular grade-level norms. Children can be seen for their strengths, rather than compared with their age mates. In addition, multi-age classrooms promote "olders" teaching "youngers," which gives children a chance to think about where they have been and where they might be going.

Team teaching adds another dimension to this community. Two adults means double the class size, which allows children a wider range of friends, role models, and interest groups than would be possible in a class with fewer students. Children and teachers know each other well, but differently than in a single-grade class. First, children stay in this classroom for more than one year. Second, Barb and Marla pool their daily observations, which more than doubles their knowledge of individuals. Third, the classroom structure they have devised provides intimate weekly time for one-on-one reading instruction—and that fosters close relationships between students and teachers. Fourth, the district mandate to find alternatives to standardized testing gives them an intellectually intriguing reason to think together about children and their work. The particular focus on assessing children's work provides another entry point to knowing students well as learners.

Marla and Barb thrive on their smooth harmonious teaming and after school they frequently sit down for an enjoyable rehash, which includes talk of the elusive and mysterious growth over time that all of us are so eager to understand. Today Marla asks Barb, "Did you see the way Tim handled that unannounced fire drill so well? Last week it really undid him." Marla talks about how proud she is of Josette for presenting her Choice work today before the group, but "she isn't there in her social behavior yet," referring to Josette's inability to attend to the reading aloud. She delights in Tita's progress in English and relishes Noah's problem solving in the construction area and that he chose to work with Ben, one of her "included" children. Then she returns to Tim, which prompts her to go beyond what she can see.

Marla has spent much of her time today with Tim, a mildly retarded child in her inclusive class. She comments about this allocation of time, expressing one of her underlying observations about the nature of learning: "I watch the strugglers more than the kids who are up and going [a common phrase in her vocabulary] who don't need my time so much. Those easy school kids like Noah are great; they are entertaining, but their learning is about them reacting with the environment. I don't know how it works that they get hold of all that knowledge; all of the sudden they make these incredible leaps. I just have to keep the environment going for them and then get out of their way."

Marla knows that children develop self-confidence when they are supported by a classroom structure that does not make learning into a contest. She tells a story to demonstrate this point, which happens to be about Tim:

"A principal from out of district came to visit our classroom. It so happened—
a fluke actually—he sat down with the three lowest readers in the group who
were all special education kids. 'Would you like to read with me?' he said.
So Tim went to the shelf and took a chapter book with tiny print. (I think
Tim thought the visitor was going to do the reading.) 'Can you read it?' the
visitor asked. Tim said, 'It's hard but I can do some of it.' The boys struggled
so he stopped and asked them how they felt about reading. 'Great,' they
said. 'We're really great readers. We can read 'is' and 'the.'" This self-
confidence becomes cyclical when children can build on what they know—
no matter where they begin. Children need this kind of self-confidence if
they are going to reach their highest potential and they need teachers who
can recognize the beauty in even their smallest steps.

Dissonance as Curiosity

On other occasions, the talk takes a more poignant tone, especially when
the world beyond the classroom intrudes. Sometimes Marla wavers about
the compromises she must make as she negotiates the Scylla and Charybdis
of children's natural development and school-based expectations, especially
on behalf of those children who fall between Timothy and Noah in their
ability to master reading and writing. She knows children do not necessarily read just because they are 7 years old and exposed to phonics. Rather,
the assumptions underlying her multi-age classroom are based on long
experience and deep knowledge of children who learn to read through
varied teaching strategies and their own unique interactions with print. That
knowledge puts her in a bind.

   She is eloquent about the constraints on variation in a public school and
how she must negotiate a path for children whose literacy achievements
cannot be hurried to match singular school norms. It pains her to decide
how much to pressure a child when she knows that her urgency to have
him master print is not in the child's best interest and she knows that the
system leaves few supports for children who are unsuccessful in meeting
the accepted time frames. The school system has a long history of classrooms
that rely on artificially constructed grade-level norms. Schools do not allow
for the individual difference that Marla knows in her heart is the human
condition. "I always have to ask myself, will the system stomp on kids before
they have a chance to become literate?" Using her hands as a vise, she describes her dilemma: "I get whomped between the system and the child when
I move kids on without those literacy skills. I let some children come to literacy later than the system permits, but some parents don't understand my
practice; they get wrapped up in getting their kids fixed. They want their
kids gotten ready—even when they aren't ready. I get my heart stomped on

frequently." When Marla acts on her knowledge that particular children will learn to read at their own pace if she resists pushing them beyond their capacity, she is putting her professional judgment and skill on the line. The compromises between what is best for children and what parents and the children's next teachers expect weigh on Marla's conscience.

As we leave the coffee house where we have spent Sunday afternoon in deep talk about children and practice, Marla comments on this ever-present dilemma of personal or external standards: "Maybe if I had my own school I would have external standards or maybe I wouldn't. I would love to let kids decide what they want to study, to brainstorm and go from there, but I can't. I am bound by what the lockstep public system says we have to accomplish."

"Would you leave to be a principal or teach in a private school?" I ask and Marla immediately returns to what undoubtedly keeps her going: "I find teaching interesting right now, especially the talk about assessment. I like the dissonance."

Genuine problems, John Dewey says in *Democracy and Education* (1916, p. 192), engage students' curiosity by creating dissonance and stimulating further thought. Certainly the problems of assessment are genuine and provoke Barb and Marla's thinking; their participation in the larger, more discordant discourse adds a deeper level to practice. (When Marla read this draft, she said about dissonance and Dewey, "Yeah, that's a Foxfire connection; that's where I got it. We read *Democracy and Education*.")

Making Practice Visible

Marla has always attempted to make her practice visible to parents, principals, and other faculty; such after-school and coffee-house talk is an important first step toward bringing any others into assessment conversation, which is—as it should be—firmly rooted in the classroom. One of the written artifacts that provides an entry point for others is a class handbook. Despite protests that she still hates to write and can't use a computer, Marla has compiled a colorful, impeccably desktopped *Class Handbook 1-2-3* to explain her complicated classroom to parents, student teachers, and the volunteers she actively recruits to work in her class. Along with such excerpts from the latest research as "Seven Kinds of Smart" (Armstrong, 1993) in the September 1993 *Family Circle*, which provides a gloss on Howard Gardner's work, Marla outlines the scaffolding for children that allows for as much self-pacing as possible in a multi-age group of 44 young children.

In the *Class Handbook 1-2-3*, students describe Choice thus: "Each day we are given a chance to play with anything in the room. We call it play but it always turns out to be learning time," and give the following advice to future students: "Have an agreement about what you are going to make if you are working with another person." "We share our plans . . . and then everyone doesn't have to invent everything all over again." Marla makes sure that children, parents, and teachers know the rationale for Choice and have a sense of the skills involved. In the handbook, Marla alerts parents that children will look like they are doing "whatever they please whenever they please." In addition to what children say, Marla's handbook addresses possible parent concerns by putting Choice in the section labeled "Creativity & Thinking Skills." A poem—without commentary—begins the section: a child whose world narrows at the hands of a teacher who leads him lockstep to draw a red flower with a green stem and that is all he knows how to do, even when his new teacher gives him a blank canvas. Next an excerpt from an early childhood text on the importance of play and the value of activities that require alternative explanations presents another rationale for Choice. The section includes a description of Choice time and a chart: "What we do and the skills we learn."

The 1993–1994 handbook prepares parents for portfolios, which are in their second year for every child. In the handbook, Marla tells parents that portfolios are a less limiting way than standardized tests to measure children's progress. She explains that portfolios are the reason work is not coming home and invites parents to the classroom to "spend some time 'visiting' their children's work." She informs them that "a portfolio is a collection of student(s) work that enables the students, teacher and others to see the efforts, progress or achievement in given areas. " To create them is not a trivial undertaking.

PORTFOLIOS IN TWO PARTS:
EXPRESSIVENESS AND CONFORMITY

Casually placed on the floor a bit away from the classroom meeting area, in full public view, accessible to all at anytime, are four large plastic boxes containing 44 folders. If not careful, one could trip over them, or miss them entirely as the physical manifestation of what is energizing teachers and provoking deep thought and talk. Certainly the placement of these boxes bespeaks the effort to "integrate teaching, learning, and assessment into students' and teachers' daily classroom lives" (Bellevue Public Schools, 1993, p. 4). Carefully labeled with names and children's current grade level circled, some are quite thick and belong to children who have been in the classroom three years. Others, representing work done in the first two months of school, are less bulky.[3] Together these four boxes form a collection that represents hundreds of tangible products from a well-functioning and richly provisioned classroom whose teachers mean to tap learning in all its dimensions. As to what she is trying to achieve, Marla says: "Those kinesthetic kids come to school and build and move and dance and then you give them a pencil and paper and they don't know what is going on. We try to make learning sensible and accessible for all kids and portfolios represent what they can do."

Teacher, Student, and Parent Selections

I choose Marienne's portfolio from her second-grade year to see what she can do. Marienne caught my eye during Choice time. She played Spin 50 and the Memory Game with her best friend, Kiki, in the kind of self-chosen 8-year-old activity that used to go on for hours with neighborhood friends after a regimented school day of workbooks, the kind of companionable play that often disappears in the modern world where working parents preclude inviting friends home after school. Marienne described these games in a whispery soft voice to a large group of peers, explicating the differences between them and designating the Concentration-like Memory game as her favorite. In her 12" by 18" portfolio folder, illustrated stories are the predominant medium and her sense of color leaps out from self-portraits and original (as opposed to photocopied) drawings.

Both children and teachers have the opportunity to choose what to put in the portfolio. Marienne has chosen to enter several lavishly illustrated stories, the invented-spelling texts of which I find mostly undecipherable. Among pieces like "How to Play Sleeping Beauty" that I cannot read is one piece chosen by Marienne that I can read. In this teacher-prompted plan for a fantasy party, Marienne writes about going with her mom and her best friend to Las Vegas for a birthday treat. The story is so detailed I do not doubt its truth, but Marla assures me later this is a purely imaginary party. Marienne's other drawings are photocopied, but these vividly colored magic-marker originals show in exquisite detail Marienne and her friend jumping on the hotel bed and eating ice cream sundaes from room service.

Teacher selections in Marienne's portfolio are the same assignments that appear in other portfolios and are more conventionally polished than Marienne's own choices. Everyone has a report on one of the 50 states; an autobiography; a Donald Graves–type "published" book with one line of text per illustrated page, a dedication, and an About the Author page; and self-portraits done in September and June. (Today Marienne wears the same pink headband that she drew in detail on last June's self-portrait.) Marienne's state report was on Oregon. In her autobiography she writes about how her Laotian mother and her Vietnamese father immigrated to America and how the family recently moved from an apartment to a house. Marla and

Barb have stapled to this final draft an entry slip with Student Learning Objectives rewritten in "kid language," an idea Marla and Barb got from Foxfire. One Student Learning Objective about self and community on this entry slip says, "I can talk or write about why people move from one place to another."

I almost skipped over a routine teacher-entered thank you note, but on closer inspection I am moved by the stark face-forward drawing of a girl that fills up all the space on the page and by the simple text: "Thank you Kiki for being my best friend." There is a business memo, a map of Marienne's room on which she acknowledged help from her mother, and a math sheet. Also included is a Pizza Hut reading promotion listing what Marienne has read during April 1993. No parent choices appear in Marienne's portfolio. Visible in this portfolio are Marienne's eye and ear for detail, her sense of color, and her ability to bring her own self to teacher-assigned work. She holds to her own standards by entering written work that does not represent conventional standards. The illustrations all have the stamp of the child. The portfolio shows convincingly enough that Marienne's writing is progressing and that school offers opportunities for her own expressive voice. The evidence from mathematics highlights the intersections between math and literacy: the child's "best" record from the pattern unit and the "best" record of free observation. The evidence for math reasoning is not as elaborated since this is a Literacy Portfolio which includes the district requirements for assessing reading and writing skills.

District Requirements—Common Tools

Along with the work that students and teachers value, the district requirements exist side by side in this portfolio. District-required writing samples are produced naturally in the daily life of the classroom, and find their way into the portfolio through a combination of teacher, student, and parent choices. The district recommends entering one writing sample per month and one student-chosen work sample per month; thus Marienne's portfolio easily exceeds the minimum eight pieces per term. But dilemmas arise when the district requests samples in formats that no curriculum would include as a matter of course. Bellevue requires three such formats, called in their language "common tools." Common tools have a short but interesting history. According to Marla, teachers on the district Portfolio Assessment Team thought that as standardized tests are "tools," any portfolio strategies for comparing students across classrooms are also tools.

The portfolio common tools grow out of the district's Student Learning Objectives (SLOs, as they are known). Unlike Provincetown, where the district guidelines specify curriculum, Bellevue's SLOs specify general competencies.[4] Broader really than the usual curriculum objectives or learning outcomes, SLOs assume more importance in Bellevue because this system adopts no reading texts. When teachers choose their own literature for reading, it is the SLOs that guide their teaching. Common tools are the link between the SLOs and the portfolios, an assessment of the district's literacy goals for children.

In 1990 the assessment team decided to tackle four Student Learning Objectives: (1) Interact/construct meaning from text; (2) Read a variety of materials to develop ownership of learning and to cultivate enjoyment; (3) Communicate effectively in writing; and (4) Engage in self-reflection/evaluation. Team members challenged themselves to develop common tools to assess these outcomes that would satisfy the district mandate for comparability of portfolios across classrooms. Marla recalls the group asking itself, "What could we put in portfolios to demonstrate what kids could do if we opened them to anyone? How could we compare portfolios—even if child moved to another school? Teachers wanted these common tools."

The team ultimately decided to link the four Student Learning Objectives to tangible artifacts in the portfolio. These four common tools "anchor" the portfolio through the following means:

1. The child's ability to interact/construct meaning from text is assessed through oral or written scored Reading Summaries and reading journals
2. The child's propensity to read a variety of materials and enjoy reading is assessed through periodic two-week books logs
3. The child's ability to communicate effectively in writing is assessed by samples of writing, including rough drafts and revisions
4. The child's ability to engage in self-reflection/evaluation is assessed through entry slips and periodic portfolio visit questionnaires.

Marienne's portfolio contains the following common tools:

1. Her ability to interact with text is based on a written Reading Summary from June 1993 on which she received 4 out of a possible 5. She apparently couldn't relate personal experience to the story, which brought her score down.
2. Evidence that she reads a variety of material comes from an (unscored) two-week sweep of her reading recorded in a reading log kept at home by parent and child. Two were done during the year. (The February reading log includes an estimate of TV watching, perhaps as a prompt to alert parents to the relationship between time spent reading and time spent watching TV.)

3. Marienne's ability to communicate effectively in writing comes from all the writing samples.
4. Her (unscored) ability to be self-reflective is based on looking at her portfolio at specific intervals from March and June 1993. During those "portfolio visits," she filled out answers to the following questions: How much do you like to read? What kind of reader are you? How have you changed as a reader since the beginning of the year? What do you think you do well as a reader? What reading goals do you have for yourself? On the back of that page she answered the same questions about writing.

Marienne's sketchy answers do not add to my understanding and I ask whether the self-reflection questions are sufficiently meaningful to children or teachers. Barb and Marla acknowledge that self-reflection is the weakest of the common tools.

Self-Reflection in the Early Years

Noah (lover of the origami folds) tells me with feeling: "I think portfolios are so important that I sacrifice my reading and writing time to show them to other classes." Noah and his friend Richard, two "olders" who have been in this class for three years, are in some demand by other teachers to introduce portfolios in classrooms that are just beginning them. In good teaching style, they take visual aids with them in the form of their own portfolios and a chart generated in a class meeting: "Why are we keeping portfolios?" This chart reflects their understanding and what kind of occasions Marla and Barb provide to support it (see Figure 2.1).

Noah's enthusiasm and commitment are unquestioned, but this chart is all about demonstrating to others; self-reflection is conspicuously absent. Barb notes that the "youngers" don't do much with the self-reflection questions on the portfolio visit questionnaire and concludes that maybe Bellevue's teachers must be missing something along the way. She has heard that Project Zero does a better job of helping young children reflect on their learning and is eager for more information. She would enjoy a visit to Cathy Skowron's classroom. But at the moment Marla and Barb are convinced that conscious reflection on work is developmental and/or that they have been working on portfolios too short a time to know how to get children to be self-reflective. Barb says: "We want to use the portfolios interactively, but kids don't use portfolios that way yet. They don't revisit spontaneously. Some kids know when it is the end of the month and time to select writing to enter in the portfolio. A small group of kids have involved parents who regularly contribute pieces done at home and those kids often are more

---

Why are we keeping portfolios?
- So parents can see what we've done in class
- To show our parents our work at conferences
- To show how hard we work in class (Is portfolio empty or almost or is it full?)
- To send to different schools when we get older to show them what work we did
- To show if you're a good student

What can we learn about ourselves or our classroom?
- What topics we wrote in writing
- You can see what friends have been doing
- Tells how you've changed from one age to another
- Helps us set learning goals.

FIGURE 2.1 Noah and Richard's Chart

aware of the rhythms of the portfolios." But, she continues, mindful that they haven't done a good enough job in this area, "I find it scary that kids in eighth grade and older often choose work for the portfolio 'only because they got a good grade.'" She also wonders whether the Foxfire notion of connecting to a real audience for work is at issue here. Except for the teaching her children have done with other classes—certainly directed at an audience—the children see the portfolios as a private matter for themselves, teachers, and parents.

At the same time Barb laments that her students don't use the portfolios frequently and spontaneously, she recognizes that "one of our goals is that kids not do work just for the portfolio or to please the teacher." She acknowledges the hard-to-resolve tension between children's propensity to meet the external standards imposed by the system and represented by what the teacher wants and reflection on their own developing standards. However, this is the dissonance that pushes Barb and Marla to figure out new strategies for more meaningful portfolios.

Student Learning Objectives and Entry Slips

Portfolios attempt to go deeper than just thoughtfully selected work samples and the entry slips that accompany children's work are one instrument that helps achieve that depth. In Barb and Marla's class, entry slips often include the Student Learning Objective (SLO) that a piece of work has met, even though the district doesn't require it. Barb is a fan of SLOs and in a phone call she explains their value, especially for a new teacher.

> The district leadership has always tended toward broad, developmentally appropriate objectives and these SLOs are indeed broad. Age ranges overlap. Then we have more specific indicators, for instance: At ages 5–7 students will start experimenting with punctuation. We went over these SLOs in the training for new teachers and I reread them frequently, at least every month or two. I think they are useful because of their non-specific developmental nature. I could operate without these SLOs except as a new teacher I would miss subtleties. I value kids enjoying reading, but I might not have thought to document that enjoyment. The SLOs remind me.
>
> I want to be accountable to parents and the SLOs give me confidence that what should be going on in my classroom is going on. Should one of the complaining parents ever have a kid in my class (the whiny parents, I call them) they could look in my portfolio and see that my kids met the appropriate SLOs. I am also more accountable because I am more organized and focused about collecting evidence.

The portfolio apparatus—what goes in beyond the actual child's work—differentiates portfolios from collections of classroom work. Many teachers have routinely kept folders as a way of storing children's work, but in Barb and Marla's portfolios, they attempt to surround each piece with enough information that an outside reader—parent, teacher, visiting educator—will be able to make sense of it. Barb points out: "The district does not require Student Learning Objectives to be listed on entry slips in the portfolio, but we do it and others are interested. Marla and I do these entry slips easily because we think about them together and because it is easier to do with our open-ended curriculum. We also believe complete entry slips with SLOs will help outside readers." For that purpose Marla and Barb have devised entry slips that accompany each piece of student- or teacher-selected work. Barb's on-line description of entry slips includes some philosophy underlying portfolios as well:

> There are three kinds of entry slips: student, parent, or teacher, depending on who selects the piece for entry. Each entry slip has the name of the student, date entered into portfolio, and reason the piece was selected. Currently they say "Who helped with this piece and tell briefly how they helped." New Standards folks use the term acknowledgements, which I now prefer because we see them written

by authors, songwriters, etc. which confirms to kids that learning rarely occurs in isolation.

Marla and I tailor-make each teacher entry slip, but keep some blank slips for spur-of-the-moment entries. For things that apply to whole class, such as self-portraits, we type up a slip ahead of time and copy it. We try to include specific learning objectives to which the project relates. Although this is not a district requirement, we feel it makes us more *accountable*.

Oh, also we put on the entry slips the specific prompt for the assignment. On self-portraits in Fall 92, we said "Make a self-portrait using as much of the paper as possible." Some kids used all the paper, but they represented themselves as two inches high and the horse and pasture filled up the rest. Our reflection on this assignment informed our teaching, and this year we made the prompt more specific: Make a self-portrait. Do not do a background. This should just show you as large as possible on the paper, or something to that effect.

It is interesting that whenever we present, even to our own staff, people want copies of our entry slips. But that's not the point. The point is, this is *our* classroom and our portfolios represent (1) *our* thinking; (2) *our* curriculum; and (3) *our* kids. Marla and I have a definite advantage being a team. We can mess about and talk on the spot about why we do what we do and that is what we reflect on our entry slips. [See Figure 2.2]

DOCUMENTING GRACE'S UNDERSTANDING

Barb wrote an account of the way emergent curriculum and portfolios support and capture a child's learning in order to convey a fuller perspective than any outsider could capture. I quote it here in its entirety.

As in Cathy Skowron's classroom in Provincetown, Barb's way of thinking about curriculum connects to what has gone before. Barb describes the beginning of the year's unit on pets:

This year's all-school integrated social studies and science topic is "World Regions and Living Things." This summer Marla and I were excited as we thought how much more real and accessible to our students this topic would be, whereas last year's concepts of space and the universe were difficult to teach in a hands-on way. I knew that I wanted to have both plants and animals in our class to make

TEACHER ENTRY SLIP (art work)

Date: _June 16th, 1994_

    We selected this _self-portrait_ to place in _Mioko_ ____'s portfolio because it gives an end-of-the-year baseline for fine motor integration and visual motor representational skills.

    Prompt: "Draw a self-portrait (a picture of yourself). Do your best drawing, and fill up this paper. Do not do a background, rather only a picture of you. Please do a pencil sketch first, then you may use marker or crayons, but you may use just pencil. You are allowed one piece of this paper. Please write your name and the date on the back of the picture when you are done."

Additional comments: _Concentrated intently on copying flowers from the shirt she was wearing that day._ (BPB)

Note "Tokyo" on socks.

Marla English/Barb Baker
Signature

Who helped with this work? Briefly tell how each one helped.
The student completed this activity independently during class time.

FIGURE 2.2 Mioko's self-portrait and the Teacher Entry Slip accompanying it

the topic of living things available right before our eyes. I have always wanted to have a class pet. Marla hadn't had pets in awhile due to allergic students and a room temperature cold enough to kill hamsters and gerbils. This was our year to try.

For the first time we created a defined "science area," and separated out some of our trade books to create five or six bins of specialty books: world regions, plants, animals, weather, and the human body. I brought in a dried sunflower, Marla brought in a live one. A student's family donated a wasp nest, and for the first few days of school "bee catching" was popular, though soon children decided in a class meeting that safety from the bees and respect for their lives meant refraining from catching them and they pledged to let go anything else they caught (mostly grasshoppers and beetles). The science table now includes hand-held magnifying glasses, jeweler's loupes, two nests, and an assortment of rocks and leaves.

Marla had an ant farm kit tucked away in the closet. She sent away for the ants. I sent away for a tadpole. We knew we needed mammals, and a student teacher volunteered two mice. We specifically chose a solid white male and a solid gray female so we could make some basic observations about genetics. We have not had such good luck with the ants or the tadpole, but the mice are a big success. Snowball has had her second litter, and we are in the adoption business, both to pet owners and to the "higher end of the food chain" (read: hungry snakes).

In her description, Barb steps back to describe an emergent curriculum, albeit one based on a schoolwide choice that she and Marla did not make. However, unlike last year's "Space and the Universe," a too-far-away concept for young children in more ways than one, "Living Things" is a natural for early elementary study. Such classic curriculum builds on children's emotional connections to animals, provides vivid experience to fuel their learning, and creates openings for raising questions, all in the Foxfire manner. Barb tells how she and Marla provisioned the classroom, thinking ahead even about the colors of the mice. They took risks with the bees and pulled back when the risks became too great. Animals died, even the frog that joined the class the day I visited. In addition to careful provisioning that provides choices for children, a safe environment, and little pressure for a particular product delivered on a schedule, the atmosphere supports children's interests. Here is Barb's description of Grace's experience with the mice, and how Barb documented Grace's growing understanding. Note particularly the way she uses Student Learning Objectives on Grace's entry slip.

Kids are keeping science logs emphasizing observation, which will go in portfolios with an entry slip that includes the District K–3 Science Learning Objectives. But documenting children's understanding is broader than that.

Grace is a new first grader of Japanese-American ancestry, just moved from Los Angeles. In our meeting just before school began, we could see Grace's linguistic talents; she was eager to tell of her love for studying world cultures and offered her animal reference books for the class to use.

On this November day, Grace chose to sign up for "mice study" during Choice, a time to clean and recreate the habitat as well as handle, for the first time, the new brood of babies born to Smokey and Snowball. The six or so children who have also chosen mice are keyed up about having eight more mice to hold. Their voices rise as mice scurry up arms and into t-shirt armholes. I remind the kids about keeping the mice close to home, and about staying calm. I head off to attend to other tasks.

At the end of Choice time, I head back to check out the writing or drawing that children are required to do as part of mice study. Grace's desk is strewn with several writings. I ask her if I may read what she has written. She sorts out two distinct works, both about mice, and hands me a "book" with stapled pages. I find a virtual "stream of consciousness" writing about the mice and their environment. The piece moves from a description of the children at mice study to a first-person narrative from the perspective of the mice. It is eloquent and moving. I am speechless. My experience from reading poetry suggests this piece clearly demonstrates Grace's deep connection to and understanding of the world around her, and her ability to express her thoughts and concerns to her reader.

Snowball
Snowball
and
Snowflake

By Grace Suzuki
November 1993

Snowballs, snowballs, and snowballs
No one, not a single person is very careful
Rough with the baby mice,
hard on Smokey
and hard on Snowball.

Poor babies.
Poor Smokey.

Smokabottoms, Smokabottoms.
Why can't they stop?
The babies are nervous.
They won't listen.
Why can't they observe?
Why touch all the time?

I am scared of big ugly faces
looking in my cage,
sometimes different
but all ugly.
Why not a little privacy?
I don't like being observed.
　　　The End

I recognize it immediately as a piece that would show portfolio visitors her true young voice. I exclaim to Grace that her piece is beautifully sympathetic to the mice's viewpoint, and in a hurried exchange ask if I may borrow it to publish right away. I also tell her I want to put a copy in her portfolio. I type it at lunchtime, copy the original and the word-processed version, and attach the copied set to a teacher's entry slip:

> I have chosen this piece to put in Grace's portfolio, as it represents her current understanding of (1) using writing to express one's opinion and feelings; (2) poetry as written genre for expression; (3) the science concept of influences on an environment; and (4) the social studies concept of personal freedom and privacy.
>
> To me, it shows Grace's already profound understanding of the cycles of life in the world. The piece was self-initiated and completed independently. I did the word processing and printing of the "broadside" [a single poem printed on a flat surface]. Signed: Barb Renfrow-Baker, Teacher.

Learning from Grace's Poem and Barb's Description

As well as exemplifying what Choice time is about, Grace's poem and Barb's description demonstrate how portfolio entries work within this classroom.[5] This portfolio entry operates simultaneously as an assessment of Grace's learning and a vehicle for Barb's reflection on curriculum and practice. (This documentation provided an occasion for Barb to write, thus adding another layer of reflection, and another important consequence.)

Student Learning Objectives add another dimension to this encounter, helping Barb think through how Grace's voice and purpose are effective communication. That Barb has them in her head (the wording is not exact) gives her an opportunity to show that Grace's literacy skills are assessed not in isolation, but along with her science and social studies knowledge. Grace's poem might have met more Student Learning Objectives than Barb listed, but since SLOs are not required, Barb did not feel compelled to look for every last bit of Grace's possible learning from them.

Barb is moved by Grace's poem, and though she thinks of portfolios instantly, which prompts her to publish the poem and enter it in the portfolio, a teacher in a nonportfolio classroom might also have rushed to publish. Grace willingly gave the poem to Barb to type, but otherwise Barb does not describe much mutuality in her response to Grace. Barb describes this in retrospect as if demonstrating learning to the portfolio visitor is the aim (and this is indeed the aim of the entry slip). Perhaps the last lines of the poem, "Why not a little privacy?/I don't like being observed," say as much about Grace as about the mice, and explain the absence of a response to Barb's exclamatory praise.

In keeping with Foxfire's philosophy, Barb and Marla want children to know that their work has a real audience beyond the teacher, an important lesson they teach by providing encouragement and various forums in which to exhibit. Grace balked at the invitation to read her poem aloud to the whole group, a public performance many new first graders forgo, but she accepted Barb's suggestion that she mount the typed copies of her poem. She worked hard and carefully chose the colored construction paper background to give to her sister and her parents. A mounted copy of the poem now hangs in the science area. The portfolio is not the only structure for saving the work, but Barb says, "If I hadn't asked Grace to keep her poem for the portfolio it might have gone home, gotten lost, never been seen by anyone other than Grace."

Barb adds, "This particular poem will always be with me." At some point she may take this poem, which has moved her so, and do a careful description of it with a group of colleagues. When portfolios provide a motivation to value children's work in a way that is all too rare in schools, the portfolios become a spur to teachers' further reflection and can provoke a deeper inquiry into practice. This poem (and other children's expressive work) is a window to the uniqueness of the child. Putting such work in a portfolio ensures absolutely that portfolios are not alike, but not all the work in portfolios aims to highlight the unique qualities of the child. Sometimes portfolios tend to make conformity visible instead—especially when the contents

are designed to show how children's work meets predetermine
form instructional goals.[6]

PORTFOLIOS FOR MANY PURPOSES:
POLITICAL KNOTS AND PHILOSOPHICAL TANGLES

When the district staff began to assess their newly revised Student Learning
Objectives, they planned for assessments to be constructed over time and
with teacher involvement, two qualities that signal Bellevue's forward-
looking stance. But there were constraints. In 1990 Bellevue started with the
hard-to-satisfy requirements that newly developed assessments must serve
both the classroom teachers and the district accountability needs. The district leadership knew it was a challenge. When the district began their mission, they took "a learning year" to consider alternatives to standardized tests
and formed three "wide-open" monthly study groups for interested teachers to consider alternative literacy assessments that would ultimately replace
some standardized tests. Independently, each group of teachers pointed to
portfolios as the solution of choice. During the second year many of this
same core group of Bellevue teachers continued to serve on what is now
called the Bellevue Literacy Portfolio Team. Marla was among the 24 teachers who came together on behalf of the district each month to design and
think through portfolios. This team defined portfolios as "both a philosophy and a physical place to collect work," and adopted a "Composite Portfolio" modeled on four distinct portfolio types developed in other places in
other contexts (Valencia & Place, 1993). The four types are:

1. Showcase—In this kind of student- or teacher-chosen best work portfolio, Grace's poem might be an exemplary piece.
2. Documentation—This portfolio might include work that shows
   progress over time and includes unique information. Marienne's self-
   portraits and other art work would satisfy this type.
3. Evaluation—This portfolio calls for standardized pieces, both scored
   and unscored, including the scored Reading Summaries, two-week
   reading logs, and portfolio visit questionnaires developed by the Literacy Portfolio Team for the purpose of aggregating data.
4. Process—This portfolio demonstrates work toward a larger project
   and would include writing from first draft through "published" book.

In the *Bellevue Literacy Composite Portfolio Staff Handbook 1992/1993*,[7] the
team is specific about the need to serve multiple purposes: "We were committed to the student involvement and ownership of showcase portfolios,

the consistency and comparability across portfolios that is assured in the evaluation portfolio, the rich descriptions of students characterized in the documentation portfolio, and the valuing of the process of learning found in the process portfolios." Working out the details of collecting that massive amount of material for each child is taking longer than anticipated.

Development—Slower Than Expected

Once this team designed the overall portfolio shape, they experimented in their own classrooms for a year, all the while hashing out with each other the details and dilemmas of the developing portfolios. Teachers in each school also volunteered to try out portfolios with the support of the original team members. Marla is the Portfolio Leader for Woodridge, the whole faculty of which has voted this year to tackle portfolios under her leadership. In other schools, smaller groups of teachers are experimenting with portfolios for the first time. Teachers from the original team and teachers who are new to this work come together to discuss common problems at districtwide staff-development meetings. As the portfolio pilot efforts spread, teachers include what they and/or their children value and ignore what is not meaningful about the district requirements. Incorporating all the common tools into each child's portfolio is at this point in the process still voluntary. Originally, this fourth year of the plan was to be more formal and the written instructions for the 1993–1994 portfolios have a mandated tone. However, teachers realize that they need extra time and are taking it on themselves to go more slowly, to "mess around more." The district is accepting this slower pace, even as they urgently need evidence for the school board to show they are moving toward the goal of the five-year plan to augment standardized tests with measures that show a more complete picture of the child. The pressure falls on the district leadership more than it does on the teachers, who are primarily concerned with their own classroom portfolios. The process is necessarily slow, but the district is supporting what teachers need. Successful portfolio implementation leaves no other choice.

Marla's Basic Belief in Portfolios with Contradictions

Pinning down the specific instructional goals and helping children reach them has always been one of Marla's own goals. "In college" she complains, "I had a teacher who always told me my work was competent, but it had no 'flair.' What is flair? I could never get him to tell me how could I get better at flair." Pinning down flair or reading comprehension or math reasoning generates plenty of the dissonance Marla likes while giving her the chance to untie political knots and philosophical tangles.

Marla has been right there participating on the district portfolio team, and as Portfolio Leader she is helping her whole school pilot the agreed-upon portfolios. Each portfolio in Marla and Barb's plastic boxes represents what they and their children decide to include as well as what the district requires. Marla and Barb have the autonomy to manage the children's and their own selections without district guidelines other than common tools. Indeed, their portfolios go beyond any district requirements. Possibly because their partnership is so generative, they have devised more mechanisms for collection and documentation than have many teachers in the district. Marla is mindful of her role: "What intrigues me is how to get other teachers to think about portfolios without adopting my models."

Marla vigorously supports the district purposes of portfolios: To improve instruction, improve student learning and ownership of learning, and report progress beyond the classroom. She adds, "If you have no basals, no textbooks, no framework where kids should be, then you have to have something." For Marla portfolios are that "something." Portfolios leave a trail of evidence that children can show parents at conference time. Portfolios provide a better source of information for teachers to meet children's needs, and for those beyond the classroom, portfolios offer more valuable data than any test score or artificial grade-level measure of achievement. And when the special education children who are so close to Marla's often-stomped-on heart come to mind, she says achingly, "Without portfolios, special-needs kids have nothing, only a test score, and some of those kids aren't even testable. I can look in Timothy's portfolio and show progress—no matter how small—that would never show up on a test." Marla also believes that "teachers need opportunities to figure out for themselves what good reading instruction looks like, and the portfolios make those discussions happen." But the closer one looks at the details of the portfolio, the more complex are the issues; standardization gets Marla right back into the vise between the system and the child.

Pitfalls of Comparing Children

As in Provincetown, the action is not all in the portfolio folder. I need guides to help me understand. I ask Noah and Richard—the proud possessors of the chart and the public speaking expertise—to show me their own portfolios for each of the 3 years they have been in this class. They each have three portfolios, all kept in large, separate folders. In their most recent (six-week-old) portfolios there are new elements that I did not see in Marienne's: a daily science log kept for two weeks and more math, a signal that Marla and Barb are broadening beyond the literacy portfolio.

Noah and Richard enjoy going through their work and we laugh as they remember. They have their favorite pieces and as we look, the "apparatus" (as I call this elaborate underpinning to the portfolio) falls away and we look at the work without the many multi-color-coded teacher and child entry slips for each subject. "Published" books in the Donald Graves process-writing manner (which appear in every portfolio in both Provincetown and Bellevue) stand out for the care taken with details of presentation. Some worksheets are routine; some details are not as advertised. Richard is missing his second-grade February Reading Sweep, a two-week sampling of what he read at home and school, and his Reading Summary score sheet is blank. "I had the chicken pox," he says apologetically.

Noah is a nonstruggler who Marla counts on to learn from his environment. Just added is a recently written letter to Food Services, complaining of the inconsistencies between the menu and the food actually served. Barb's handwritten teacher entry slip illuminates Noah's writing skills and how he did the work. She notes his "empathetic self" and his "passionate" voice when he talks about the letter (see Figure 2.3). Still, his Reading Summary of a narrative does not receive a top score. Marla acknowledges that this common tool task does not tap his strengths: "He is not a narrative sort of guy," Marla says, but a scientist and mathematician, a reader and collector of information, not a storyteller. Score aside, the imprint of the child is definitely present. Family is evident everywhere, perhaps the most striking aspect of Noah's collection. Noah writes of family trips and family history, and his parents' help is credited on many entry slips. His parents have written several entry slips recording why they value a particular piece of work. Do I know Noah (and his family) better from this short portfolio visit? Absolutely.

I then look at Tita's portfolio with her. I have spent time during class with Tita, who is chewing gum against the rules despite having been told by at least six children to spit it out. Tita writes on my Powerbook: "wndpsthgm." Marla passes by and reads the invented spelling without blinking: "We're not supposed to chew gum," congratulating this Spanish-speaking "older" for her typing. Tita has emigrated from rural Mexico and had not been to school before she joined this class two years ago. In response to last year's imaginary party prompt, Tita wrote about her birthday party and richly illustrated the story. She asked me to read it to her twice so she could remember and then after listening twice she read it back to me. Out of all the pieces in her portfolio, she took the greatest pleasure in reading this story and pretty much ignored the rest (see Figure 2.4).

How does one assess Tita's interactions with text? Certainly not on a Degrees of Reading Power (DRP) or a California Test of Basic Skills (CTBS).

TEACHER ENTRY SLIP

Date 10-15-93

I selected this piece of work to place in Noah's **portfolio**

because it demonstrates writing for a meaningful purpose; the editing
process; and current understanding of business letters.

Additional comments: Noah expresses his empathetic self with this letter.
As he talks about this letter, his voice is passionate.

Barbara Baker

Signature

Who helped with this work? Briefly tell how each one helped.

Ms. English helped them clarify their thinking, and she and Ms. Baker

helped proofread and offered standard business conventions.

Richard did the initial input to the computer and both students shared in

proofreading and editing. They shared the job of addressing the envelope

to be put in the school mail.

Woodridge School
12619 S.E. 20th Place
Bellevue, WA 98005

10-1-93

Dear Food Services,

Some kids in this school district cannot buy lunch when you
change the schedule, because they cannot eat certain foods. Example:
I am a vegetarian. The schedule says cheese pizza. When I go to buy
lunch, I see that it is meat pizza. I cannot eat it. If it is possible,
we would like you to serve what is on the schedule. When you do
something like box lunch, we'd like to know exactly what is in it
[especially for free lunch people because they have no other choice.].

Sincerely,

Richard Oaks

Richard Oaks

Noah Richter

Noah Richter

FIGURE 2.3 Noah's letter and the Teacher Entry Slip accompanying it

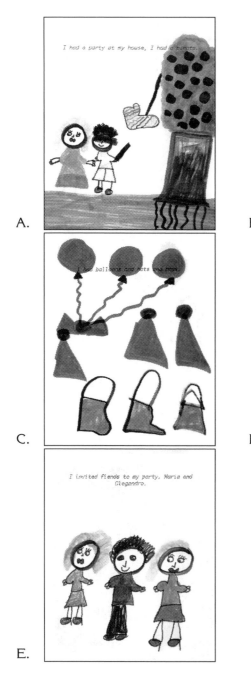

A. I had a party at my house.
   I had a piñata.

B. I had juice and cups and
   enchiladas.

C. I had balloons and hats and
   bags.

D. I had cake and I had presents.

E. I invited friends to my party,
   Maria and Olegandro.

FIGURE 2.4 Tita's favorite portfolio piece

But what information will a Reading Summary score tell anyone, except that Spanish-speaking Tita and English-speaking Noah show disparities in their ability to summarize district-chosen English reading prompts? Tita's reading log is blank, perhaps because no one at home could help her or maybe she, like Richard, had the chicken pox. Certainly both Tita and Noah deserve the same opportunities for education and teachers have the same obligation to support their learning, but comparing them with each other within the same time frame neither gives the teacher more information nor helps Tita master English faster. Tita can't go faster than she is going. She is a child who gets caught in Marla's vise because her pace does not match the system's uniform expectations. Comparisons of children perpetuate the notion that school is a contest with winners and losers. This Reading Summary, standardized as much as possible, does not take into account the various ways children enter print. Certainly common tools are not sufficient to give a complete picture. Still, the Reading Summaries attempt to make conformity visible without any particular benefit to the individual or the teacher. Will the scores on these summaries be useful to the district? It is still an open question that depends ultimately on how reliable, valid, and comparable the summaries turn out to be. Nancy Place, the district leader of the assessment project, points out that the purpose of the summaries is to support instruction: "The teachers have found it useful to develop criteria for what makes a good Reading Summary and their discussions continue to provoke conversation about teaching kids to read."

Reading Summaries: Standardizing a Nonstandard Task

In Provincetown, Cathy Skowron used the *Legend of Sleepy Hollow* summaries to document children's "facility with language," recognizing that synthesizing three versions in writing might—just might—yield information useful to her practice. Across the country in Bellevue, the impetus for similar language documentation comes from district needs rather than teachers' curiosity. The hottest, most energetic portfolio talk I heard surrounded Bellevue's Reading Summary. One of the four common tools in Bellevue's portfolio, the Reading Summary attempts to measure this Student Learning Objective: "Interacts with texts to construct meaning." Bellevue's Reading Summary raises some of the same language questions Cathy was trying to answer in her portfolios.

In the Bellevue *Portfolio Handbook*, the Portfolio Team acknowledges that evaluating how children interact with text is difficult and that it is impossible to "see" children's interaction with text until they write or tell what they have read. It is also hard to judge the difficulty of text. "The level of text that kids can comprehend is the knottiest problem," says the district language arts specialist. Reading abilities, the handbook says, are a function of the reader and the text, so reading performance is variable. The teachers and the district leadership have designed an assessment to address these three complicated, intangible, interrelated aspects of literacy. Barb and Marla have agreed to try out the district's pilot version of the Reading Summary before the district mandates its use. Reading Summaries are "in development."

During my visit Barb spent the reading period with individual children summarizing district-provided narratives. Every 20 minutes I watched her sitting close to a different child in a cozy space on the floor helping that child master this task, but found the dyad too intimate for me to intrude.

Later, Barb explains these tête-á-têtes. Since the purpose of the Reading Summary is to assess how a child interacts with text to construct meaning, Barb tries to remove every variable except summarizing. She reads the story if the child cannot read: "The purpose of the common tool is to assess the ability to summarize, not to demonstrate the physical act of reading." She takes dictation if the child has trouble writing, since "this is not a handwriting sample." She makes sure the child knows all the vocabulary, since "this is not a vocabulary test." She gives children a chance to connect to prior knowledge, since "children need to have all the information to do a good summary." She stops at the end of each page to make sure children are holding information in their heads. Sometimes she reads the passage twice if that is not too boring or the child reads it once and then she reads it.

"My first question to the child is 'If I ask you to do a summary of a story, what does that mean?' I try to elicit the difference between a retelling which would be a lot of details and a summary which is about the main ideas. If we are reading from Arnold Lobel's *Frog and Toad Eat Ice Cream*, I ask 'What do you know about Frog and Toad? What do you know about ice cream?' And since the story hinges on understanding that ice cream melts in the heat of summer, I ask questions like 'When do we like to eat ice cream? What happens to ice cream in the heat?'" After children summarize the text, Barb asks, "Does the story remind you of anything else?" which is to elicit a personal connection. She asks if they need to add anything else or if what they have said or written makes sense. "If someone else reads the summary would they understand the big ideas in the story?"

In order to score the summary, Barb looks for recall of important information and whether the child draws inferences, gets the main idea, constructs a personal response, and demonstrates a coherence that communicates the essence of the text. The day I was there Barb did not score the summaries. Scoring is not yet mandated, though when they are scored, Marla takes that information back to the district meetings for discussion.

Barb raises some issues small and large. A problem that no one foresaw when the district chose the developmentally labeled reading passages is that many children have seen the *Frog and Toad* videos, adding another variable to how accurate the measure of children's summaries of stories about these particular amphibians is. And then there is the nature of narrative. Barb says, "Sometimes I prompt as the story frame suggests which is 'The story began when_____, then _____, and finally_____.' I know that encourages kids to see the story in thirds, whether the story is naturally or instrinsically in thirds or not." The biggest issue is standardization: "We know that what is important for me may not be important for you, yet we still ask kids to come up with the same main ideas. In my studies of anthropology and art I picked out details that fit in with the meaning of what I was creating for myself; I knew that some of what I thought important would not be relevant to others, but it made sense for me and for what I was studying. I imagine the same thinking applies to children's summaries."

When I raise my caveats—that children's ability to summarize what they hear taps different skills than what they read, and that the ability to construct a personal response is not connected to the ability to do a summary—Barb reminds me, "Hey, remember, this is only a pilot."

But her description raises issues that bedevil all efforts to standardize tasks that are basically nonstandard. A phrase that showed up often in her descriptions is "Depending on the child." As she immediately pointed out, "If I proceed exactly as the district recommends and the procedure doesn't fit the child, I naturally change my strategy. That may elicit a better summary from the child but doesn't provide a similar measure for comparing other children."

Standardized Portfolio Scores and Standardized Testing

Scored reading summaries are only one effort to meet the school board mandates for measurement. Scoring whole portfolios is next on the district agenda. The scoring issues bring the question into focus: How much can a portfolio be expected to do? These portfolios represent what the child can do for an audience of parents, children, and next teachers. They are used as an assessment tool in addition to tests. They affect staff development as teachers learn from them. They are meant to provide aggregated numerical data to evaluate the programmatic effectiveness of language arts in the district. The aggregating of portfolio data is technically not to give a child a score. The score is not meant to get back to the child, but to provide a way to say something about a group of children—for example, that based on portfolio work, some percentage of third graders have met a specific

SLO. It may not be important that a specific student is a "3." Yet aggregated data may or may not overload the agenda for portfolios. It is conceivable that if scores become too codifed and too prominently attached to portfolios, then the district's purposes will eclipse the local aims of displaying the knowledge and progress of individual children. Conversely, if the district has no stake in the outcomes of portfolios, they may cease funding the professional development opportunities for teachers.

As ambitious as these aims are, they are still anchored in what is possible. The school board's goal is not to replace standardized testing with portfolios, but to provide another source of evidence for achievement. However, there is a national propensity for policymakers, administrators, parents, and even teachers to embrace numerical measures and standardized answers. This result of standardized testing over the last decades is hard to shake, no matter how good Bellevue's intentions; numbers are easier and more efficient to read than complicated evidence of human variation. Though the Bellevue school board may endorse the notion that a more complete picture of the child comes from an unscored portfolio than from a single standardized test score, the board is still wedded to information about the language arts program delivered in numerical form. They want to know "how our fourth graders are doing in reading." Therefore, no matter how beneficial the portfolios are without scores, the scoring proceeds to satisfy the school board.

Over and over the district has made clear that the purpose of scoring portfolios is not to evaluate individuals, but the underlying fear is that if such numerical evaluation becomes possible, the school board will welcome it. A year after this visit, reports are that portfolio scoring has reached a reliability of .7, considered appropriate for assessing program effectiveness but not individual children. The reason given for not reaching a more reliable score is that the portfolios are not standardized enough. The argument in Bellevue about scoring continues to affix itself to how standardized the portfolios can or should become. In general, teachers fall somewhere between Barb's distaste for considering individual scores and Marla's recognition that there might be a temporary benefit. At the moment, more and more teachers are implementing portfolios and the scoring of individuals remains in the background.

Despite the school board's hunger for numbers, Bellevue's assessment policies are more humane than places where kindergartners repeat the year based on one standardized test score. Standardized tests in Bellevue are not as ubiquitous as in many districts—except for Special Education and Chapter I children, who come under federal regulations. (New federal Elementary and Secondary Education Act [ESEA] legislation will alleviate some of this testing.) Children designated for programs supported by federal money are tested every year from kindergarten on. "It's sick," Marla says. "That's one of our big goals to use portfolios for these kids instead of tests." In a relatively enlightened policy, no standardized tests are given to most children until fourth grade, when students take the California Achievement Tests in reading. Their scores are published in the newspaper by district, not individual school, which is a kinder, gentler way to record scores than many cities and states adopt.

Beginning in third grade, Marla and Barb must give a district-made criterion-referenced math test to assess how well they are doing in teaching to the Student Learning Objectives. Marla says, "That information is good and tells me in what strands I am not moving kids." No decisions are based on these scores, which come back to teachers and then go home. They are entered in cumulative files in the office but not in the portfolios: "We don't put them in portfolios for reasons of privacy."

No matter that other places have it worse, scoring portfolios raises the question for Barb of whether scored portfolios are any better than testing. She is eloquent in an on-line argument against scoring—even as she, like others, takes the focus on the individual as larger than it is technically meant to be. Her written comments highlight the personal nature of her classroom, where the threat of scores can cause a teacher so much angst:

> Are portfolios and performance tasks and detailed rubrics just creating a different way to rank kids? I heard Ted Sizer ask that question last year at a talk in Seattle. If so, then I agree that we best rethink our intentions.
>
> Three years into my teaching career, I already have some definite feelings and opinions. As Bellevue begins to "score" the whole portfolios we've piloted for up to two years, purportedly for information on how district objectives are met, I fear for my students. I fear that whoever ranks them with this scoring system won't know that Johnny's personal life is a wreck, that he frequently doesn't eat dinner, that he clings to Joe's ideas and expands upon them to make them his own. I think I (and Johnny's parents, were they interested in doing so) would make the best assessments because they and I know him. And if I'm the best qualified, then why score and rank in a more formal way at all?
>
> As for my own accountability, I actually feel more accountable with the portfolios right in front of me, particularly with the "entry slip" system Bellevue has implemented. Every piece in the portfolio says why it was selected, and acknowledges who may have helped with the piece. I can write on the slips which district or state (or potentially Goal 2000) goals they meet. I like having standards to shoot for and

to tell my kids to shoot for (Foxfire tie), but the reality of it is, my ESL kids, my mildly mentally retarded kids, my Johnny with the wrecked home, they may never meet the standard.

Right now, with our inclusive elementary school model, they are successful. But I don't look forward to the day when I have to tell them, or watch them find out, that they didn't meet the exemplar's standards.

When I read Mem Fox's *Radical Reflections—Passionate Opinions About Teaching, Learning, and Living* (1993), I became engrossed in her conjecture that the affective connection with a human being is so vital in the learning. (Also ties to Foxfire's memorable moments— human interaction is often one of the common qualities of great learning experiences.) So why can't I just teach and help my students LOVE learning? I am the one they'll remember (I hope); I doubt anyone remembers their 3rd grade CAT score. I love our portfolio process, but I love it because when Johnny and his mom and I all sit together we find joy in what he has accomplished, that it is "good enough" because he has made progress. Frankly, I don't care how other children score compared to Johnny.

Marla is more willing to live temporarily with scoring: "We are mandated to score portfolios, but we also are mandated to have portfolios that demonstrate who the kid is. When you get more parents saying, as they are beginning to say to teachers now, 'You really know who my kid is,' that response feeds into the cycle. More teachers will see the value of portfolios and then the scoring thing will slip away." She thinks that this standardization is a necessary step along the way toward the day when the public trusts the teachers and the portfolios. "The more teachers come to value what they can learn about children from the portfolios, the less they will need the scores. But right now the need to score stands out, even though no decisions are based on them and the board never intended that scores be attached to individual kids. Scores are only to inform children, teachers, and parents through the district data." Marla sees that scoring could be the thin end of the wedge to use scores to make decisions, but she is willing to let go of this issue for now.

The actual scoring is not a task close to Marla's heart. Neither Marla nor Barb volunteered to join the group that did the pilot scoring. This year, those teachers who have piloted portfolios have met once to score. Marla says about this first experience: "I don't know how I feel; I need to play with it more. Our group got high reliability, but it doesn't help me to know a kid is a 3 on a rubric of 1–5. If it tells the district how kids are doing in reading and reduces the reliance on test scores, I will support standardiz-

ing some things in the short term to get people to see the value of portfolios." But she raises an issue from her test-and-measurement background:
"I wonder if a certain percentage of kids score '3?' Will portfolios break
down into bell curve when the goal is to move *all* kids?"

Marla does believe the exercise of scoring has some instructional benefits: "We each put our own scores on a pieces in sample portfolios, scored
the whole, and then talked about it. There were traditionalists in my group
who asked about every writing-process example, 'Where is the brainstorm
list?' and scored down for its absence. The 'rowdy constructivists' like me
wanted to look at development over time. But we all learned something by
looking at what kids could do and figuring out what could they say about
it." The scoring raises another issue for Marla: "Should K–1 portfolios look
different—be more open-ended, since kids can't read yet? Could we adapt
them to make these portfolios look more developmentally appropriate?"

Many of those who think about portfolios are asking the same question
asked by Nancy Place, the Bellevue District Language Arts Specialist: "Can
we use classroom-based assessment, portfolios in this case, to give program
information without destroying the very thing that makes the classroom-
based assessment so valuable: its particularity, its reflection of the individual
child?" Nancy makes a plea for an open mind: "We have to try this scoring.
Otherwise we don't have any information for the school board." But she—
like others—believes that until policymakers accept teaching and learning
as a complex operation, "we will get nowhere in our understanding of how
to help students learn what they need to succeed."

ENGAGEMENT IN THE COMPLEXITIES OF
TEACHING AND LEARNING

Portfolios honor children's learning styles—which is a gigantic leap away
from standardized measures. Many believe the best way to identify those
styles is to look at children's work and talk about it. Bellevue's portfolios
have opened up the opportunity for teachers to do just that.

A New Teacher Talks About Reading Summaries

I am first introduced to teacher talk about Reading Summaries when Carla
Hein comes to Marla and Barb's room at lunch to share her students' work.
A second-year kindergarten teacher at Woodridge, Carla brings responses
to *Rain*, a picture book by Robert Kalan and Donald Crews (1991). Catching Carla's contagious excitement about the five drawings and their dictated
retellings, Marla and Barb go through them one by one and speculate about

the evidence in the drawings that children understand the story. They probe possible inferences about how the child interacted with the text. Carla is thrilled, not only by her realization that children listened and made meaning of the story, but that she saw how they made the story their own by changing a detail or drawing one element to the exclusion of others. The variety of children's responses is visible right there on the table. Also implicit in this exchange is the question of what is involved in reading instruction, and an even deeper query—what is reading, really? Marla is genuinely excited by this conversation and Carla's initiative. She points out rhetorically, "Under what other circumstances can new teachers discuss their practice over lunch without it having to be about a discipline problem?"

Engagement at the District Staff-development Meeting

The next morning I go with Marla to a half-day district staff-development meeting, one of a series of four, reaching a total of 120 Bellevue teachers. Barb and a regular substitute cover the classroom. Barb will attend the afternoon session. Thirty teachers at a time are released to bring two portfolios and discuss, as the overhead put it, (1) how to implement portfolios and (2) learning to look at what portfolios show us about who children are. The meeting is jointly run by Nancy, the District Language Arts Specialist, and Sheila Valencia from the University of Washington. In 1990 when this assessment effort began, Nancy asked Sheila to join her in figuring out what to do. Nancy's background in progressive education and the Prospect School's methods of Descriptive Review and Sheila's background in literacy and educational measurement represent two very different approaches to assessment. Both perspectives prove necessary to fulfill the school board's charge to find alternatives to standardized testing that include measures of comparability, reliability, and validity. The staff development they do reflects the stamp of their differing perspectives.

The kitchen-table arguments between Nancy and Sheila encapsulate portfolio evolution in Bellevue and are a running story line through the whole process. In introducing the plan for the morning, Nancy unfolds the argument they had at Sheila's kitchen table while planning for this meeting. Sheila wouldn't sit still for just "What does the portfolio show about the kid?" She wanted the prompt to be "What does this portfolio show about the kid in relation to the Student Learning Objectives?" Neither of them would give up a favored framing question. Finally, in a breakthrough, they divided the agenda into two different lenses for looking at the same portfolio to accommodate what they know is the "healthy tension" between Sheila's focus on instruction (what the teacher does to help children move forward) and Nancy's emphasis on knowing the child. They remind the group of their own heated, valuable, and public conflicts. Nancy encourages everyone "not to be polite" if they disagree with each other. Sheila and Nancy make clear throughout the meeting that teaching and learning are complex and negotiated enterprises, whether in staff development meetings or in the classroom.

The teaching profession does not usually provide occasions for teachers to examine their practice, make explicit their assumptions, or analyze the complexities of practice with colleagues, but here the connections between the adults are electric as they tease apart their portfolio practice. During the part of the agenda devoted to questions and comments, questions about Reading Summaries come up at once. "What kinds of language do you use to elicit summaries?" someone asks. "I'm convinced it matters what you say for what you get back." A first-grade teacher describes how she has children fold a paper into thirds ("a lesson in itself") representing beginning, middle, and end to prepare them for seeing the shape of a story, which leads to a discussion of the developmental nature of this summarizing task. Marla says, "Last year kids could do oral summaries, but this year when they know how to write them, they revert to retellings." The question arises whether to put out models (synopses of *TV Guide,* for instance) and teachers wonder what to do when children summarize what is important to them rather than meet the standard of a good summary. The discussion broadens to the perennial portfolio topic: the pull between showcasing "best work" and putting in "the good, the bad, and the ugly." A teacher thoughtfully muses, "What happens if I teach a bad lesson, do I trash the kids' work as well?" and answers her own question, "What kids choose keeps it real." Teachers may think the child's choice is a "wart," but the child may understand that it is a step along the way—or, another more cynical teacher wonders, is that child just being strategic by putting in a "wart" to be able to demonstrate impressive progress at the end of the year? "Sandbagging," he called it.

Carla's talk from yesterday about Reading Summaries continues. It spills over into break: Is this response to *Rain* a retelling or a summary? Does the critical difference between them matter in a simple story appropriate for 5-year-olds? Does pushing children to state the main idea detract from their personal response? Is personal response necessary to get a high score or is such a response a different matter entirely from the ability to summarize? If a child has a lot of prior knowledge about the topic, does this Reading Summary measure the level of complexity of text he or she can understand? The district provides six or so graded Houghton Mifflin stories for two out of the three required summaries during the year. The third can be the teacher's choice based on her own or a child's selections. How does that constraint interact with the child's preferences? Do the Reading Summaries leave enough room for the unique qualities of the human mind, especially if teachers are going to score the summaries?

After a break, teachers look at portfolios in small groups across grade levels. In the first session Nancy asks teachers to note what they can say about the child from looking at the child's work. Teachers fill out a sheet: "Who is this child? What can you tell us about the child's strengths, weakness, kinds of knowledge, dispositions, preferences? What could be included in the collection that would help [the teacher] see more? What opportunities would you recommend be provided for this child in the classroom?" Reading Summary score sheets help here not at all. Teachers look at what children include and what they choose to write about or draw (and rigid classrooms where curriculum is teacher-controlled are visible in an instant).

Next, the group shifts the lens to Sheila's focus. Using the same portfolios to focus on instruction, teachers look for evidence that the child's work meets the district's subject-area instructional objectives. Again, it is hard to get a handle on a child's reading skill, though one can see enthusiasm in a child who keeps a complete list of books read and a rich reading journal. Complexity of text mastered is hard to judge. Wonderfully clear is how much teachers learn from each other, even on basic logistics: "Is that how you do your reading log? . . . . Wow, you put first drafts and final drafts in. I'm going to do that." Teachers share curriculum ideas ("Those are terrific pop-up books. How did you get kids to do that?"; discuss how to make portfolios more meaningful to students ("My kids don't like the reading logs. How can I get them to be more enthusiastic?"), and talk in detail about a kindergarten child's two words on a paper, which in fact represented a long sequence of choosing a book, reading it, and talking about it in front of peers, along with this initial effort to write. The child exerted much more effort than was evident from the portfolio entry. The talk around the portfolios started out tentatively—who knew what would show up in this first opportunity to share portfolios? But discussion took off quickly and the common task readily lent itself to a collaborative focus on children's work rather than on a comparison of a new teacher's portfolio with Marla's. (Which is not to ignore that the new teacher exclaimed at break, "Am I ever going to be able to do the kind of portfolio Marla does?")

Back in the large discussion, a teacher asks a perennial question—"Since I don't teach older kids how can I tell what is good work?"—and others make the point that it is hard to tell what is good work even at your own grade level. Teachers acknowledge the need for advance, explicit, public criteria to set standards, and that they have the responsibility to help children meet those standards. "It is not enough to to expose kids and expect that they will learn. We have to help them." But questions arise: Where do standards come from? Who sets them? Marla points out that children must be involved in standard-setting. The good-natured group goes back and forth without consensus, recognizing the messiness of the issues. They discuss whether they liked today's groups mixed across grades or prefer to be with teachers at their own grade level. Is it too competitive/anxiety-provoking to show your portfolios at this early stage to teachers at the same level? Or can you learn more from a colleague who teaches same-age students? The group recognizes the courage and trust it takes to open their portfolios (and hence their classrooms) to new colleagues.

So accepting is the response to this sharing that a reluctant teacher who previously held back a child's work hands the pass-along portfolio to the next teacher right on the spot.[8]

A teacher volunteers that she is keeping a portfolio of her own teaching and that her students are interested in what she is putting in it. Sheila adds that the University of Washington is now asking students in the Teacher Education Program to keep portfolios. Someone jokes, "Do they have common tools?" Sheila responds, "If I'm involved, you know they'll have common tools." And the discussion touches on including the common tools in classroom portfolios. Nancy and Sheila emphasize that portfolios have to be meaningful to teachers or they aren't worth the effort, but they also know that the district purposes bring pressure.

The Reading Summary may be the most problematic of the common tools. Reading Summaries have the same potential for abuse as any standardized measure, whether teacher-generated instruments in a portfolio or multiple-choice items made up by some distant expert test constructors. Though no teachers might ever have thought to devise a Reading Summary on their own, this common tool provides opportunities to engage seriously with colleagues. In the process, teachers learn, practice improves, and children benefit. Marla thinks that the common tools do not constrain teachers, but rather begin the process of talking to each other. This meeting, just one sliver of portfolio talk, confirms what is increasingly clear: Teachers' talking to each other is essential for professional growth. Whether they talk about the nuances of summarizing the main idea of a story or begin from experiences in their own classroom or describe children's work, teachers learn. Further, if teachers have opportunities to articulate their practice and grapple with the hard issues themselves rather than leaving outsiders in charge of the agenda, they will get better at delineating what is at stake for children and for their own teaching lives. They will contribute to the wider debates on assessment, tracking, equity, and national standards. Marla is clear that Reading Summaries are only one entry point to assessment discussion and cites the provocative conversations teachers have about the process of reading. She maintains that the scores do not yet get in the way of that talk.

Looking at Children and their Work: Descriptive Review

Marla had never been a student teacher; she came from a child-development background and her methods courses advised her to read scope and sequence charts and textbooks to figure out how to teach. She never looked at children or their work. "When I actually began to teach in special ed classrooms, I learned to look. The kids couldn't tell me so I had to figure out from their work what they understood." For Marla, looking carefully at children and their work with colleagues has been a high point of the Bellevue assessment work, perhaps the most important consequence.

When Nancy brought the work of Descriptive Review to Bellevue in the form of a voluntary study group for teachers, Marla connected. The underlying purpose of the study group was to provide teachers an opportunity to think about the assumptions underlying assessment. (Valencia & Place, 1993). For two years, Marla (and later Barb) joined other teachers each month to look at children and their work according to the collaborative processes developed by Patricia Carini and her colleagues at the Prospect School in North Bennington, Vermont (Prospect Archive, 1986). Like the Project Zero Collaborative Assessment Conferences used in Provincetown, these processes teach how to look carefully at children and their work, and do this looking in a group.

One of the Prospect documentary processes, Descriptive Review, works like this: The chair poses a focusing question to the group. This question frames the teacher's request for feedback and recommendations that illuminate some puzzling aspect of the child. The process then specifies that the presenting teacher (and often the presenting parent) describe the child fully, rendering physical gestures, temperament, relationships, formal academics, and interests in as detailed a way as possible. After this uninterrupted presentation, participants ask questions in formal turn-taking order to clarify the description of the child's experience. In the next go-around, the group offers recommendations for practice, always building on the child's strengths. Finally, the group considers whether the session respected the child and the family. The formal go-around makes space for every person's voice.

The particular kind of looking matters. One central goal of Descriptive Review is to stay away from judgment or evaluation; the aim is careful, balanced description of the child. Descriptive Review builds on children's strengths rather than lamenting their shortcomings. Over time, teachers develop detailed, shared knowledge of particular children and come to articulate their own questions, their own teaching values and standards, and to recognize children's own standards. This ability to look carefully and describe throughtfully is central to the utility of portfolios. After all, what is the point of collecting work if you don't know how to look at it? Or if it does not help to keep the child at the center of your focus?

Marla found Descriptive Review transforming: "I keep a lot of what I know about children and their work in my head. Descriptive Review gave me a better process of getting at this. I wasn't very good about articulating what I knew about each kid—I knew it inside me—but I couldn't help someone else observe what I saw. Descriptive Review gave me a way to discuss and share my observations. I now go through those categories (physical presence, emotional tenor, relationships, academics, interests) while I'm in the shower. I think about kids who have slipped away, who I have big questions about, who are struggling. I use the categories and try to figure out what to do. Then I make time for those children in my day. Thinking about kids like this is a habit now."

This engagement in inquiry is essential if standardization is not going to be the ultimate result of all this portfolio work. "I said I would try the common tools so I have to have them in the portfolio, and the hardest part is the time." But the time issue has a deeper edge than the usual complaint. Marla elaborates on where the portfolios have taken her: "We are committed to looking at kids' math process, including getting them to solve an open-ended problem with many solutions. That kind of close attention to math reasoning requires a one-on-one situation. The more I get into doing it, the more time I am desperate to have. Barb and I are pulling more and more kids for longer time, but we want it to be even longer. We have stretched our student teachers to the limit to get that one-on-one time with kids to figure out what does math reasoning look like. Like reading, it happens inside of kids, but I need to make it explicit. If I don't figure out what that math reasoning or reading looks like in my classroom, people outside—administrators, researchers, policymakers—are going to tell me how to teach math based on some other conception of learning that has no connection with what I know about kids and curriculum."

Although standards are often comparative and pegged to grade-level norms, Barb and Marla believe that that does not have to be the case. But Marla cautions that doing without comparative external standards is possible only if teachers are articulate and can explain their practice. She regrets that many new teachers and even experienced teachers do not know how to observe children or know enough about what kind of instruction learning to read requires. In Bellevue the development of portfolios helps teachers understand more about instruction and gives them opportunities to make their practice explicit.

No matter where the conversation goes, Marla and Barb have their eyes on the child. Marla always returns to children who struggle and how they get squeezed by the system. "The portfolios help me show their performance is higher than a standardized test, but it is a Catch 22. If only other people would accept children the way they are, but above my level that doesn't happen. When they get to fourth grade, kids are all supposed to be on grade level." "But," Marla continues, "we are just beginning to address these issues on a district level—it is going to take some time. We don't know the accountability part yet and that will become clearer as we get more practice. Teaching has always been something you did privately in your room with kids. Portfolios make it more public, but not if they are just dumped on teachers. We are still searching."

This search on behalf of children is the reason Marla and Barb arrive before dawn and leave after dark.

CHAPTER 3

Portfolios at Fenway

A Moral Tug of War in an Urban High School

We work on deadlines. We have to. We need kids to succeed in real world performances, not just get good grades. We need to look at their products and ask did the kid perform well? We have to set policy for everyone, but we have to make room for the kids who don't fit the mold.

—Mildred Sanders

The setting is the doorway to Mildred Sanders's classroom at 3:00 P.M. Tenth-grade Fenway student Janet Hamilton gets Ms. Sanders's attention by laying down a gauntlet: "Boy, is this school in trouble."

"What's the matter?" Ms. Sanders answers calmly.

"Well, my mother is going to be on the warpath when I get home and tell her what's happening here." Ms. Sanders waits. Janet continues, "Nobody teaches here." Pause for drama. "Teachers are supposed to put up a math problem on the board, do examples with us, and then have us do more of them at our seat." Pause. "When my mom gets through here, you better be careful."

Without a word, Millie (as adults, but not students call her) motions to Janet and her friend to come into the classroom. She positions them in front of the bulletin board and points to the Coalition for Essential Schools' (CES) *Common Principles* (see Appendix B) posted on the wall and reads aloud: "The governing practical metaphor of the school should be student-as-worker. . . . a prominent pedagogy will be coaching, to provoke students to learn how to learn and thus to teach themselves."

Decidedly unconvinced, Janet says: "Teachers get paid to be the workers, we don't." Millie, known for her equanimity, ignores Janet's provocative stance and points to Principle 1: "The schools should focus on helping adolescents learn to use their minds well."

"Yeah, yeah," Janet says, having made sure that Millie, a trusted teacher, hears her tirade. She leaves for home with her friend, and I predict she'll be back for another talk tomorrow, without her mother.

This mid-October visit to the Fenway School on behalf of Four Seasons has brought me to Mildred Sanders's classroom door to record just such evidence of the new relationships between teaching and learning that mark school restructuring. The purpose is to document how Millie thinks about these questions: How do we know students are learning? How much and what do they have to know to reach an acceptable standard? And what happens to students who do not or cannot meet the standard expectations? What is fair and equitable? Who decides and by what right?

Though it went through my maternal head to suggest that Janet go to her room, and were I the teacher I would have been hard put to avoid a contest of wills, Millie was perfectly confident that Janet would learn from this exchange. That stance fits Fenway's atmosphere—and Millie's faith in students. Restructuring—the taking apart and the putting back in a rearranged relationship what happens in schools—is Fenway's self-chosen calling.

High schools are notoriously entrenched in tradition (Sizer, 1984), and how far Millie—and Fenway—has moved from the norms of a large comprehensive high school is one thread of this complicated story. Although the primary teachers portrayed here face the same issues in delineating standards and worrying about how to help those who don't meet them, when students reach the secondary level, the stakes are higher. Standardized testing looms larger. Concerns of jobs, money, and children of their own crowd the classroom. The dilemmas facing elementary teachers pale beside the immediacy of Fenway's quest. Be forewarned: Like the other teachers portrayed here, Millie aims to document her students' learning and capture their growth over time, but the story of Fenway's secondary school assessment efforts—fraught with society's harsh realities and messy attempts at democracy—go well beyond a description of Millie and her classroom.

NEW RELATIONSHIPS IN A RESTRUCTURING SCHOOL

The striking point about Fenway Middle College High School is the uniformity of the student response to the question of what is important. "People here are friendly; we know everyone." In *Speak for Yourself,* an impressive 1992 student publication of photos and text, the human touch leaps out—dramatically. The photos are not always about hugs, yet they bespeak car-

Today, Fenway is made up of about one hundred eighty students and eleven faculty members, all creative and dedicated individuals. They provide an intimate and caring learning environment that makes the school different from any other: in other words, The Best. ❖

Thomas didn't Know much about Cameras so I Took him under my wing And Showed Him How to fly.

FIGURE 3.1 Sample selection from "Speak for Yourself"

ing and warmth; they show students and faculty who like to sit, stand, and study close to each other. This insight about the Fenway community is not unreported. In March 1992, *Teacher Magazine* featured a story, "All in the Family," by Mary Koepke, with the lead "Kids in Boston find a home away from home in a school that tends to the heart as well as the head." This statement made about many early childhood classes would hardly raise an eyebrow—except perhaps in Madeline Hunter's behaviorist school where parents were told "You love them; we'll teach them."[1] But Fenway still tends to hearts in a high school where teachers must educate against the odds, and students are of an age when failure to achieve academically has increasingly grave consequences for their future lives.

I find it dramatic to enter the subway in historic downtown Boston and emerge from underground to see a stark high rise, seemingly dropped out of the sky onto an expanse of available space. Others must find it so as well, since most accounts of Fenway begin with this vista. I arrive off the "T," as the Boston subway is known, six stops north of Boylston Street, in Charlestown on the Boston Harbor. *Old Ironsides* is visible off to the right— but only on a clear day.

The Charlestown Naval Yards—bastion of the Irish working-class familiar to many from Anthony Lukas's *Common Ground*—have been rebuilt with medical facilities spun off from Massachusetts General Hospital and other small businesses. Economically, Charlestown is a good place to locate industry. The residents tend to be laborers; the firefighters and police families have moved on. But none of these demographics determine who comes to Fenway. Located on the cement campus of the Bunker Hill Community College, this easy-to-reach alternative school draws its 185–200 students from all over Boston.

No measure of economic need exists for these students since free lunch is not an option for their high school, despite one faculty member's estimate that 90% of the students would qualify were it offered. Approximately 14% of the students have children of their own. A majority work, Millie says, and more would like to work, but can't find jobs. Though the school keeps no official records, an administrator suggests that 60% of students work full-time.

The student body is diverse. Standard categories do not sufficiently represent students' rich ethnic and racial heritages, but the school reports that approximately 54% are African-American, 22% are Latino, 22% are white, and 2% are Asian American. Another dimension is the mix of "first-chance" and "second-chance" students. First-chance students, often the "best and the brightest," come to Fenway's new heavily funded ninth-grade CVS Pharmacy Program to prepare for health-related careers or for the small intimate environment offered here. Sometimes they come from another comprehensive high school by choice. A former Boston school superintendent's child, now at Harvard, attended Fenway for two years. Second-chance students sometimes have dropped out of parochial or prestigious schools that require an exam to enter, or have been kicked out of regular comprehensive high schools, or have had trouble with the law, or are returning from interrupted schooling with children of their own. School guidance counselors and savvy insiders who know a good opportunity for students are the major conduit for information about Fenway. Applicants are taken on a space-available basis.

The school works hard to build a common culture and to avoid stigmatizing students for past failures or previous absences from school. The carefully crafted mission statement mentions "safe, supportive, and ethnically and culturally diverse environment . . . personal attention and nurturing, independence and responsibility . . . encouragement to think critically, pose moral questions, care for others and participate in self-government." My notes are full of details confirming this. Yet these lofty goals, which Fenway accomplishes with impressive high morale and panache, do not mention a whole set of academic aims, unquestionably the traditional province of school. The moral tug of war between what Fenway knows it does well and the need to "get kids to do academic work" is the locus of the school's own struggle. This tug of war between the mission statement and academic achievement is not about winning and losing; everyone is holding on—somewhere—to the same rope. This Fenway story is about ambivalence. Though ideally both humanistic values and academic rigor can coexist, individual faculty members go back and forth as they argue with themselves. The reality of shifting circumstances causes them to see the merit of both sides at once and at the same time lament what is lost when either academics or emotional well-being gains ascendance. A taut rope connects both sides of the argument. The push-pull tension between Fenway's choices charges the atmosphere with purpose.

Cultures Crossing

The Fenway community would readily agree that the heart and the head highlighted in *Teacher Magazine* (Koepke, 1992) do not occupy a hierarchical relationship, with one more valued than the other, but they admit that balance is hard to achieve. When teachers look through Fenway students' eyes at today's kaleidoscopic world, they see that the solid old values about how school works have melted into air. Those students, teachers, and parents who have experienced large comprehensive high schools with their emphasis on basic skills may not recognize what Fenway is about. The yellow triangle traffic sign on someone's doorway—"Yield: Cultures Crossing"—is not just about multiculturalism.

This new world view calls for new thinking, negotiation, and compromise. When teachers help students understand the ways knowledge and meaning are constructed and create environments in which different languages and kinds of knowledge are valued, then students stand a chance of connecting to academics. In order to accomplish this task, teachers must give students more voice in their own learning. They must put students at the center of their education, and relinquish some of their traditional power over school standards and evaluation. This shift requires major change. Fenway is attempting no less.

I arrive at school early to find the acting director deeply engaged with a student over a computer screen. This senior (one of 48) is having a "private advisory" to help him get over a hurdle that might prevent his graduation. He has no classes after lunch except his required advisory. Though he has no good reason for missing this class, rather than let him fall off the edge and drop out so close to his goal, the school meets him more than halfway by providing this alternative solution. One could see this as too accommodating or, in a different light, as a chance for him to have some personal before-school time alone with an adult in authority. This ability to bend, yield, negotiate, and see the world through other eyes is absolutely necessary at Fenway.

Networking Knowledge

Unlike the situation at many new magnet or alternative schools now springing up in the fertile ground of school reform, the administration at Fenway does not control the hiring. Faculty are hired in the same manner as other Boston teachers. Fenway's veteran teachers have "done the heavy lifting for themselves over the years" says Larry Myatt, the founding director, describing the labor of realizing a shared vision. But hard issues still weigh on them, especially in the matter of assessment. They ask themselves relentlessly: How can faculty evaluate students' growth *and* hold them to standards of knowledge—especially if notions of arbitrary standards and content are disputable? Ten years after the school's founding, this question continues to precipitate heated debate. Fenway does not bury its head in the sand; the administration has seen to it that faculty have abundant professional-development opportunities to participate with others who are thinking about these assessment questions. The faculty welcomes the chance to engage in the national debates.

Fenway's association with three sometimes overlapping national school reform networks exposes faculty to the newest ideas about assessment. Millie Sanders is a Coalition of Essential Schools National Faculty Citibank Fellow, which allowed her to spend a summer month at Brown University team-teaching high school students, collaborating with teachers from across the country, and learning about systemic school change from Coalition researchers. The purpose of this national faculty is to form a cadre of CES teachers who can work with new members as they attempt to restructure their schools. Representing the Coalition, Millie has been a member of the Four Seasons Project since its inception, bringing her Coalition expertise in schoolwide reform to that network and returning with assessment knowledge to support her Coalition colleagues. Extremely energetic (and energized by all this professional activity), Millie is also part of the Fenway math team, which consists of four teachers plus Linda Nathan, Fenway's associate director (on child-care leave) who functions as math team facilitator. Together this team has thrown itself into a new adventure—they are learning to teach the reform-minded Integrated Math Program, which includes rigorous training and a heavy dose of portfolio assessment.

Each network brings some experience with assessment to the discussion and Millie draws from all of them. But no matter how heady these experiences, and how much the latest thinking about assessment contributes to her teaching, Millie is more passionate about students' welfare than she is about the latest educational buzz words. How a particular assessment will promote Janet's growth is Millie's central question. The Coalition's emphasis on student exhibitions of knowledge and mastery of skills, the math portfolios specified by the new curriculum, and the authentic assessment featured in Four Seasons are all in her head, but she is clear: "If portfolios full of student-selected math work and exhibitions of what students know will help them in the world outside the classroom, I am all for such assessments." Otherwise, she'll skip them. Millie feels strongly the imperative for her students to reach beyond rote learning and education as seat time and connect what they know to real life. But she will move mountains to help students meet more traditional academic goals, including the standardized reading tests students must take to graduate. For Millie, the ceremony of portfolios is to enhance students' work habits and celebrate their visible progress, but, because she is a pragmatist, student portfolios are not yet an invitation to delve into the mysteries of students' mathematical thinking.

EYES ON THE CHILD: A SPECIAL EDUCATION CLASSROOM

Put out of your mind a large high school class facing the blackboard and an impersonal teacher lecturing for the 20th year from a textbook, without regard for student response. In a squat portable module that houses some of Fenway's classrooms on the Bunker Hill Community College campus, Millie teaches several classes of 8 or so, and once daily works with another math teacher to teach a larger group of 25 ninth graders. They share their strengths—his in math and hers with individual students. It is an imaginative organizational structure that supports them both. Students sit at round tables in working groups. Vestiges of the textile art from last year's artist in residence are still on the wall. A row of IBM computers sits ready for use. No one would mistake this for an early childhood classroom, but it is closer than the usual bare high school environment.

In Millie's after-lunch class, eight special education students work on basic skills independently or with a student teacher (who happens to be expecting triplets, which adds a note of interest to the situation). Millie has the luxury of spending her time interacting with individuals rather than a

FIGURE 3.2 Millie Sanders and a student

group and her relationships with students reflect that focus. As she teaches, she is continually asking herself, Did a student not understand because he didn't do his homework? Didn't ask questions? Didn't realize he didn't understand? Tuned out? Either she or the student went too fast? Millie's understanding of obstacles that students face dictates how she intervenes.

Today Millie spends the entire period with Ronnie and Elisa. Elisa has just returned from lunch, for which Millie lent her money without a qualm, but with the expectation of prompt, full repayment. Though Elisa is not yet focused on the math and complaining about the quality of the lunch, she already has her materials out when Ronnie sits down at the table. Millie's style is warm and students gravitate to her, so I am not surprised when Ronnie waits without proposing to do any work. I ask if he is her advisee, assuming this might explain his presence, since advisees often appear at odd times for consultation. "No, I'm her son," he says, with a big smile, claiming kinship by skin color as he puts his brown arm next to hers to demonstrate a match. A particularly mature looking junior, he is enormously charming. Millie ignores his attempt to be family (he is not) and asks him to get out his math, demonstrating how she relates to students. She is open and accessible, but tough; the message is joke with me—but I expect serious work.

Coincidentally, both Ronnie and Elisa use the same pattern blocks found in all the classrooms I've visited. The four of us sit at the table working out geometry problems from the new Integrated Math Program curriculum using these variously shaped blocks to test our solutions. These hard problems engage Millie and me as well as the students in figuring out the rule for how many individual squares it takes to build an increasingly high pyramid of blocks. But though the ostensible topic is curricular, Millie has another agenda. Ronnie has learning difficulties, and Elisa, a ninth grader, has behavioral problems that frequently show up in special education classrooms. According to a career program form Elisa shows me, she has an intact family with a middle-class income and high academic expectations. She herself has well-defined career aims to help deaf people learn to speak. She is also interested in sign language. But she has few social skills, friends, or connections with peers—except as she annoys them.

She annoys Ronnie today with a steady stream of talk about his girlfriend, but that is the price he pays for Millie's help and company. He says to the table at large that Elisa is a pain in the ass. Millie reminds him that last year he was a pain in the ass and that both of them are going to work together. "You'll be her mentor," she says as she begins to execute a long-term plan for their mutual education. I realize that though I have been focusing on the regularities of pyramids all period, Millie has been promoting student-to-student connections, reminding Ronnie how far he has come, holding out progress for Elisa, and doing the substantial work of promoting each student's personal growth. Fenway faculty will argue that without these connections to each other their particular community cannot flourish academically, that academic growth cannot take hold in a socially sterile environment. On another day, however, the same faculty might worry about their students' missed opportunities for total academic focus, since students have so much to learn.

From Business Ed to Special Ed

Millie didn't start out as either a special education teacher or a math teacher; she is an emblematic example of personal transformation. She began her teaching career 20 years ago in the only public postsecondary business school in Boston, and took on the role of reform right from the start by insisting on replacing comptometers (old-fashioned fancy adding machines) with calculators. When that school became part of the state system, in order to retain her city seniority she became a business teacher at a large high school. First, she moved the typewriters so students could interact and not spend their class time facing the wall. When the principal requested that she move them back, she replied through an intermediary, "If you want them back, you move them." They stayed, and she stayed, putting into place a five-year plan to update the technology and the teaching methods. But even with the team teaching she arranged, the school was still rigid. As she taught, she became intrigued with how she could help the special education students gain the necessary skills to succeed in school, and went back to the University of Massachusetts for a degree in special education. Millie came to Fenway four years ago as a business teacher, but when a special education slot opened up, she was ready to take it.

In her first two years at Fenway, Millie joined the humanities team; for the last two years, she has been a special ed teacher on the math team. She had no particular background in math and the mathematical knowledge required to participate in the math team's intensive curriculum development was admittedly a stretch for her. She switched because, she said, "kids have the most difficulty with math and they need the most support. And the person who provides that support has to 'get' the math in order to help the kids." She sees herself supporting students in ways that she couldn't in humanities. "Humanities is easier and not so specialized. Sure, I could see that they did their work and help them read, but I felt that math was holding them back even more than reading." Being on the Fenway math team has enabled Millie to have regular conversations with her colleagues around "big ideas" in mathematics, and her excitement is palpable.

After school, I go to get my things out of Millie's classroom cabinet, and a student is opening the combination lock, which startles me, since why would one lock things up if students have the key. "How did you know the combination?" I ask not exactly kindly. "It's my lock," she says. Only later when Millie tells me her own daughter attends Fenway do I make the connection—and connect to the fact that Millie has entrusted her own child to Fenway.

THE WORLD BEYOND SCHOOL

Real-world Lessons

The emphasis at Fenway is not always on academic skills, no matter how much students need them. School life is designed to provide purpose and motivation beyond the subject-based classroom. What is extracurricular at other schools is decidedly and consciously curricular at Fenway. I sit in on a yearbook meeting. The teacher who advises student government has arranged for a member of Fenway's outside advisory board to join the meeting. A long-time supporter of the school, he agreed to help five student leaders make a business plan to pay for the yearbook. Sitting in a row behind a skirted table that covers their sneakers, the students face this dark-suited gentleman whose sneakers are fully visible. Marlon is the initial speaker. Well-prepared and articulate, he presents the choices the committee has to make about size, color, and quality. He fears that compromising, especially on the number of color pictures, although it would bring the price within reach, would cut down the number of buyers. In response, this businessman engages all five students in thinking about how to lower the price dramatically and still have a top-of-the-line yearbook. "Persuade every single student to put up $10.00 and when you've got every student's money in your hand, tap corporate sponsors for the rest. Call me when you're ready. The president of the bank down the block is a friend of mine and I'll set it up. He'll get the competition going. Once he contributes others will." This man, who is white, mentions that the bank president is black, letting his audience take in that successful businesspeople are not always white.

Someone suggests getting recommendations from students about a proposed printer, and Marlon replies in the same confident tone of voice as the businessman, "I recognize one of the girls in the sample yearbook from her picture and she's a friend of mine. She's at B.U. now. I'll call her tonight." I ask Marlon later what he learned from this meeting. As he rushes up the stairs to class, he snaps back an answer not found in a textbook: "Networking counts." From the top of the stairs, he turns around and adds, "I learned you gotta break down the task. That's important."

Fenway provides other real-world lessons beyond the classroom. This ethnically and racially mixed full-time staff (two African-American women,[2] one African-American man, two Latinas, one Latino, three white women, and two white men) recognizes the need for connecting students to role models with whom they can identify. Right after the yearbook meeting, Fenway holds a school assembly planned by the Latina acting assistant director to celebrate Hispanic Heritage Month. Three Latinos have been invited to speak to the whole school: a female school administrator who is a doctoral candidate at Harvard, a recent male Dartmouth Medical School graduate, and the Harvard-educated male head of the Boston Housing Authority. Students sit by advisories in a large banked college auditorium. A poised African-American student moderates (another student tells me the planner wanted a non-Latino to make the program diverse). Six students have written introductions for the speakers in Spanish and English, and acquit themselves well in the delivery. The invited guests are practiced inspirational speakers and tell tales of adversity, hard work, and success. They talk about how there won't be so many dark-skinned people in the real world as in this auditorium, but "don't let that stop you."

I am inspired, but the effect of this assembly on the students is not easy to read. It is two minutes to dismissal and time for questions. There are none. I am surprised, but also aware that students have been warned not to leave until the program is over, even if it runs past three o'clock. The next day, Marlon perceptively explains to me the lack of questions: "The program was wound too tight for Fenway. We're used to things being looser. We knew these were important people and there wasn't an opening. They spoke one right after another. Questions depend on the air in the room."

Real-world Questions

The "air" might not have been conducive to questions in that assembly, but as schools go, the "air" crackles at Fenway as adults wrestle with immediate and long-term challenges that students bring to them each day. The next morning in D108, a large room where teachers congregate and all have desks (but share only two telephones with long cords), they talk to each other and the outsiders (a grant-funded documentor of exhibitions, a student teacher, a potential student teacher, and me) with an intensity rare in schools. The joint office seems to contribute to the electricity of the atmosphere.

This morning a senior is preparing to go off to a Bunker Hill Community College Algebra II class, which is a "cool" privilege in some Fenway circles, but points to another thread in the tangled skein of how best to educate Fenway's students. Millie's special education students feel taking college classes is "nerdy." This difference in attitude adds another facet to the job of connecting Fenway students with the world beyond school. Building an inclusive community at Fenway requires a balancing act that would daunt many schools. Faculty struggle with how to include an amazingly wide range of students in the same untracked student body. Some Fenway students are academically inclined and connect easily with school. Others value the particular experience at Fenway but do not make an effort to master the academics. Still others like school and want to stay but struggle mightily with the work. Fenway commits itself to accommodating all these students and providing them with multiple entry points and a shot at real-world success. That task presents high challenge.[3]

It is in an energetic conversation here that I first encounter the metaphor of portfolios as "capital," like money in a savings account or treasures in a safe deposit box. Teachers collect ongoing portfolio work and lock it up in their classroom file drawers. Provincetown's whole room full of cumulative portfolios and Bellevue's boxes casually left on on the classroom floor for all to see contrast sharply with this secondary school policy. The message to these high school students seems to be that finished work is valued and that locking up work keeps it safe, since a portfolio left on the subway is no portfolio at all. But the security measures also keep students from copying other students' completed work. The same method that honors portfolios also prevents dishonesty. Nothing is ever simple at Fenway.

Yet pleasure in work is visible. Today is the due date for the Humanities exhibitions. When the students arrive, their excitement mixed with nervous tension spills into the office as they come to show adults their work and seek last-minute advice before they present their propaganda poster campaigns to peers. Conversations with students supersede adult conversation. It is not that students interrupt, but that the adult response to students' genuine enthusiasm for this school task takes precedence.

My goal during this office visit is to examine the Senior Exit Portfolios, which are an important connection to the world beyond school. These Senior Exit Portfolios are analogous to official transcript files at other schools. I choose a June 1993 file at random and am startled by the honesty of the file, compared with the usual carefully cleaned-up, but thin, official records, or college application packets. A successful case, this student has gone on to a good historically black college. In her portfolio, she has vividly detailed her unhappy experience in a highly touted racially integrated junior high program where she was bused to the suburbs, and felt "watched all the time." She describes her problematic junior year internship at Fenway, explaining and reflecting on the less than stellar recommendations she received. Her unofficial SAT scores are buried deep, along with her insightful comments on them. Her file presents a convincing picture of a strong, honest young woman who would add vigor to a college campus.

Whether any examples in this portfolio stand up against the polished, crafted writing that can be done by students in a more explicitly academic environment gets at questions educators often ask. Does quality writing depend on devoting diligence and discipline to academic skills at the expense of valuing character and honesty? Or is it abrogating responsibility not to prepare students to compete in conventional academic arenas, since those skills are still currency in the mainstream world? Can both goals be accomplished without diluting either one? Fenway's balance between head and heart does not make for easy choices.

A Special Ed Success Story

Like Marla at Woodridge, Millie is Fenway's consummate advocate for students who are different, who are caught between their own developmental path and the rigors of the system. In Millie's case, the bureaucratic vise can force students out of school—a serious consequence that Marla does not have to face. Millie proceeds stoically and practically. Just as she has a strategy for promoting Elisa's and Ronnie's personal growth, she has an action plan for the director of Fenway. By his own description, the director of Fenway sees his role as "quality controller and conserver of staff energy," and Millie wields her own effective hammer when she goes all out to see that the system doesn't beat students down. The director readily admits to appreciating her forcefulness and tells his own stories about rethinking his stance in the face of her persistence.

Millie tells a story to illustrate what happens when she bumps up against authority, which also underscores how she succeeds with students:

> I had a child whose parent would never sign the permission to be tested, even though her daughter had some kind of of learning difficulty. Finally the parent agreed to everything but the psychological test, and it turned out she was a "point 3" (the number of periods she should be out of the classroom having special help). The director said we couldn't have her here. But I felt that was unfair. I didn't think you should eliminate a child for a learning disability. My strategy to convince the director was that every time this student's name came up in a staff meeting, I said something good about her—like she was really good at interacting with people, or she can really follow oral directions, or she is really good at following through, or teaching others, or maintaining a good attendance record. I never let up. True, when it came to it, she couldn't read very well and her writing wasn't that great. But I figured if she took word processing all year, she would learn something; after all, there is a relationship between reading, writing, and word processing. The director said she had to go back to English High, where she came from. The child said, "I'll quit school if you make me go back." The director didn't want that on his head.
>
> Well, she finished the program here in three years instead of four. I'll put her up against any regular ed kid. With my help, she really learned to access the system. I took her to the library and connected her to a friend of mine, a black librarian, to make sure she had help when she needed it. I taught her to make sure she took tests in a silent room. But when it came time to take the standardized Degrees of Reading Power—you have to have a 64 to graduate and you can take it twice—I knew she couldn't do it in a large group setting. She had trouble filtering out all the stimulation. The director said she should take it the first time around in a group. I fought for her under the special ed regulations that said she could take the test untimed and in a different space. She got an 85 on her first try.

Both Millie and the director are proud of this story, and there are more more stories like it. In fact, Fenway lives by stories.

MATH A NEW WAY

A faculty member tells this story about a new Coalition school that has just changed its schedule to allow 90-minute periods for math: "The teacher is panicked: 'What do you do in 90 minutes? After I've gone over the homework problems, taught something new, and the kids have practiced it, I still have 45 minutes left.'" The Fenway math teachers listening to this tale of reform gone awry have a good laugh. "No wonder they don't know what to make of their extended period. They haven't changed a thing about their old math curriculum." Fenway, with its 75-minute periods, has changed everything.

Fenway has no ordinary math program. Their current curriculum grew serendipitously out of a past event. Two years ago, the faculty began to develop its own math curriculum with the support of TERC (Technical Education Research Consortium), a technical assistance consulting firm for hands-on math and science learning. But as hard as the faculty worked and as much fun as they had, the students proceeded faster than the curriculum. Students were ready for a second-year sequence before the faculty developed it. Building on some fortuitous coincidences and impressive networking connections, Fenway fell into an attractive option to be the first Massachusetts school to pilot the Core High School Mathematics from Interactive Mathematics Program. IMP, as it is called, was developed by high school and college math teachers at San Francisco State University and the University of California at Berkeley. Fenway faculty acknowledge they would not have been ready for IMP without the experience of trying to develop their own curriculum. Now, even though IMP is developed far away from Fenway, the math team feels they own the curriculum, undoubtedly a factor in their enthusiasm. Curriculum without such ownership is often doomed to failure.

Inquiry for Teachers *and* Students

IMP is a distinctive piece of school reform, written in response to the National Council of Teachers of Mathematics standards. IMP integrates all the math strands, thus avoiding the tracking implicit in maintaining different math courses, and calls for open-ended solutions and student writing about both math reasoning and group dynamics. Students are asked to reflect on their own learning and to consider their own and the group's process. IMP includes hands-on experiences and sophisticated thinking about mathematical ideas. Students can enter it from many levels of mathematics skills. IMP doesn't depend on memorization for success. Teachers and students often sit down together with the same answers and compare their different processes; the emphasis is on reasoning, not the result. This curriculum is work in progress, and in October 1993 students work from pamphlets that say "Draft printed 7/6/93." But most intriguing, though a teacher's guide exists to help with the mathematics ideas embedded in the problems, there are *no* answers given. Implications of this no-answer-for-teachers program are powerful. The training is serious, intense, and buttressed by collegial support. Teachers cannot teach this program by rote. There is no teacher-proofing here. Problems appeal to all ages and teachers genuinely engage in working out their thinking, which has got to inspire students to follow their lead.

When I was at Fenway, a perplexing problem came up from the homework paper "Thinking with Numbers:

> *A Fractional Life.* Demochares lived one-fourth of his life as a boy, one-fifth as a youth, one-third as a man, and then lived thirteen years more. How long did this gentleman live?" (Patterns in Mathematics, 1993, p. 19)

Before school, Millie discusses the problem with a student teacher, who has already gone through it with her husband. Then she checks it out with a colleague and math mentor. "It's 60," he coaches, "$1/5 + 1/3 + 1/4 = 60$." Millie persists, her eye characteristically on how the students will perceive the issue: "But the last $1/4$ is life as a man, so that would equal 60 and the last 13 years might be beyond that." Millie decides she will accept either answer if the students can make the argument. "It all boils down to interpretation, and I am sure Kevin will see the ambiguity and challenge me. It would be just like him." After school she checks out her thinking with the visiting math consultant and tells him how students responded in class. Kevin did indeed challenge her in front of his ninth-grade class, and she did accept his alternative answer, even though now she sees more clearly why the answer is 60. She has modeled a true spirit of inquiry because she is so engaged in the process.

MATH PORTFOLIOS: YEAST IN THE SCHOOL CULTURE

Fenway, situated on the campus of an institution of higher learning, offers students a chance to succeed not only at high school, but in college—if faculty can just get "it" right. The "it" in this case—teaching and learning—may encompass the student's entire life at times. Urgency to get "it" right, especially when dropping out is a legal option, pushes the teachers forward. Figuring out how to connect students to academics so they can capitalize on these opportunities keeps Fenway's faculty awake at night. The knottiest questions right now are precipitated by the newly emerging portfolio practice. Portfolios activate the pressing discussion around the gap between what students value and what the faculty would like them to value. Portfolios also starkly accentuate the key dilemma: How can standards be personal, idiosyncratic, and tied to the uniqueness of each individual and simultaneously be the same for all?

At the moment, portfolios act as yeast in the Fenway school culture, a physical catalyst for collegial talk about how to get students to value academics. Portfolios leaven the assessment discussions throughout the school and release potent energy for talk about change. Portfolios are still in transition. Faculty know that for portfolios to become as personalized as the rest of Fenway, teachers must move them beyond the current adult-graded folders that hold samples from students' completed term's work. But the unsolved question persists: How do we combine the most fair and equitable judgments with support for students' academic growth? Portfolios have not yet yielded answers that satisfy Fenway, but the presence of portfolios in the school culture has caused teachers to change irreversibly the way they think about the relationship between curriculum, instruction, and students. The fact that the math team facilitator is doing her doctoral thesis on the effects of math portfolios on teachers may be relevant here since it adds another layer of interest to the ongoing discussions of portfolios. She has been periodically interviewing teachers and this two-way exchange of knowledge and information fuels the effort to figure things out.

Fenway's changes have been in process for some years; like yeast, they required the right conditions to begin. The move from total reliance on standardized tests and multiple-choice exams to portfolios depended on several interrelated circumstances of structure and temperament: a hard-won freedom from many of the system's bureaucratic snarls, a stable faculty open to new ideas, and strong, energetic administrative leadership. Several more conditions sustain that change, among them faculty willingness to join national networks that expose them to new understandings of learning, a safe collegial place to test out growing knowledge about relationships with students, and encouragement to try different strategies in the classroom.

Changes away from standardized measures free faculty from teaching to the tests and allow them to uncover a wider range of student strengths and differences than can be captured by a single numerical score. One result is that teachers look at individuals rather than seeing the whole class as a single entity. Not all changes are due to new assessment practices; the systemwide Coalition-prompted improvements are intimately related. Until the number of students each teacher saw each week was reduced by half, it was almost impossible to talk about seeing individuals. Once teachers hold several students' interests and differences clearly in focus, they can't return to planning the same curriculum for an entire class and relying on the same standardized measures of achievement. Recognizing student differences necessitates curricular changes, since teachers begin to plan for particular students rather than some modal composite student. More personalized and more diverse teaching strategies for learning engage students more directly and enrich the learning community teachers are trying to build.

Currently, portfolios stand alongside other measures that compete for student and faculty attention—like SATs and DRPs, which neither help students learn nor help teachers plan for learning. But even as they see the benefits of the new assessments, faculty—more than the administrators—are convinced of the importance of tests. Standardized test scores have never been highly valued at this alternative school, either by the administrative leadership or by the students, who see college SATs and their ilk as yet another institutional inequity (Velvel, 1993).[4] Generally, due to faculty encouragement, 70% of the students sit for the SATs once, but do so without any test preparation, even when it is offered (Southworth, 1992). Teachers, more than administrators, feel the keen responsibility that students must pass the standardized Degrees of Reading Power in two attempts with a score of 64 before they graduate. The administration is less constrained by the school's final exams, and has always been on the lookout to replace them. Four years ago, through a combination of administrative and faculty efforts, Fenway abolished final exams in favor of exhibitions and portfolios. Since then some forms of portfolios have existed at Fenway, but the more recent math portfolios require the faculty to undertake the ongoing, slow, confusing process of figuring out these new assessments.

Millie tells a story of a quantum leap in faculty understanding:

> After I returned from the 1992 Four Seasons Summer Institute, I brought back a definition of portfolios from Giselle Martin-Kniep: "A purposeful collection of student work that exhibits the student's efforts, progress and achievement in one or more areas. Student participation in the selection of portfolio items is essential." The staff liked this definition, which was later published in *Holistic Education Review* (Martin-Kniep, 1993). None of us really understood what portfolios could do but we started working from that definition. Then the discussion shifted to planning what goes into a portfolio. I kept saying, "Where is the student input? Don't students get a choice?" People were skeptical about students getting to pick. "Pick" was the

word that kept coming up. They kept saying, "Well, if kids are going to pick what goes in, they could skirt around the work by picking only what they have done." I suggested we confer with each student. "No time," they said. Then I insisted, [and Millie's vehemence conveys the strength of her feeling as she repeats what she said a year ago], "It will be a teacher's portfolio, not a kid's portfolio."

Linda recalls, "Millie came back from the 1992 Four Seasons Summer Institute so charged up. The day she whipped out a definition of portfolios and said with real passion, 'See, it's not about the teacher deciding. It is the interaction about the work between the student and the teacher,' she became our 'portfolio expert.'"

Students do pick the work to put in their math portfolios, but even so the curriculum and the culture of Fenway conspire to make math portfolios rather standardized affairs. The portfolios do not take away from the basic beauty of the curriculum, which requires new relationships between teachers, students, their work, and each other. These collections, which have letter grades attached, provide a physical place to store completed work, and thus qualify as portfolios, but they mainly provide a springboard for faculty talk about students and their work. Talk with students about the work is not yet as developed as is possible. A physical place and an impetus for teacher reflection may be more than enough to ask of portfolios, especially in the first year of this innovative curriculum.

IMP specifies the portfolio structure and the structure of the written reflections. For each unit, students select two *favorite* problems of the week and two *important* pieces of homework/class work that represent key mathematical ideas. Students write cover letters for each piece that describe what they learned and why they chose it. Millie emphasizes the separate cover letter or write-up for each piece, perhaps to highlight the sheer amount of writing students do. The assignments are straightforward, but I am struck (even as I try to describe the math I observed) by how hard it is to write problems clearly and how much revision and thinking about language it requires. IMP emphasizes the ability "to state the problem in your own words clearly enough so that someone unfamiliar with it could understand what you are asked to do. Describe how you went about solving the problem. Did you find any patterns that helped you? Was this problem too easy, too hard, or about right? Explain why. What did you enjoy about the problem? What didn't you enjoy? What about the problem would you say is 'doing mathematics?' ; 'doing arithmetic?'" How important this writing is to the students is unclear. The faculty has yet to tap the possibilities for using it as a window to student thinking.

Each term students write a cover letter for the entire portfolio, which must include how they progressed in working with others and presenting their work to the class. If they haven't done their work for the unit, the responsibility for it doesn't go away; they still need the complete work for the term portfolio. Thus, Millie emphasizes, the portfolio is an aid to consistent production, a structure for supporting students' developing work habits. Millie is clear and unconflicted about that. Other issues for Millie and the faculty are murkier.

Grading Portfolios—A Ritual in Common

In her first year of managing these portfolios of student-selected work, Millie is convinced that grades are the biggest problem. The dreaded grading "is a school measure of performance, not a real-world measure." She tells me the administration doesn't like portfolio grades and is pushing to get rid of them. But every portfolio gets a grade, "for no useful reason." Millie says students like grades and expect them, so with her characteristic pragmatism, she accepts them for the moment.

The math team meets together weekly during school time to grade individual pieces of student work holistically. It is perhaps Fenway's version of Descriptive Review as used in Bellevue or Collaborative Assessment Conference used in Provincetown. Since it is not the end of the term, no IMP portfolios have been graded yet. It is not clear to me whether this collaborative exercise is to aid in grading individual portfolio pieces or to get a handle on grading the whole portfolio. I am told, "You're confused because we're confused." In any case, Millie describes the process of holistic grading the way it is done on the Fenway math team: "We sit together each Tuesday to look at work in portfolios. We all look at a piece of work and give it a score from 1 to 5 and then compare our responses and discuss the differences. Then based on discussion, we negotiate a score. We have to convince others of our thinking. It's a slow process. Then when we assess students on our own, we can tell how far off we are from the group." Millie appreciates the opportunity to look at work with colleagues, even if the portfolio grades are useless for her own assessments. She makes a final point about how insignificant the grades on individual pieces really are.

A better reason for this grading ritual is that it gives the math team a common task around which to gather their thoughts. Millie believes the discussion of student work uncovers children's difficulties. This joint looking helps teachers figure out what students are missing in their attempt to meet the IMP requirement that they rewrite problems in their own words clearly enough so that someone else could solve them. Through these weekly meetings, faculty members have seen that many students have trouble with this task of explaining the problem in their own words. The piece of work on the schedule for the next holistic grading meeting requires the student to find patterns of squares on a checkerboard. The paper suffers from a lack of mathematical ideas, but the problem may be a lapse in clear writing rather than a flaw in mathematical reasoning. The faculty may not see it that way. The relationship of language to mathematical reasoning and the IMP emphasis on verbal and written explanation is not a "hot" issue or one the faculty is willing to probe deeply. At the 1993 Summer Institute, Millie's colleague Paul Harrison argued that "we have to know if kids can really explain mathematical ideas in words," and Teachers College Professor Clifford Hill rebutted that "kids may be drawn to mathematics precisely because math is so elegantly nonverbal." Paul didn't agree. Millie does not see students' difficulties with reframing problems as a language issue either. "Not really." she says. "Students just don't understand what is important about the original problem." Clear prose requires hard work and revision, a value that goes back to the real-world question of where Fenway puts its energy. Would they really want students to use their math time for revision of writing or to be doing more math? What would have to be sacrificed to accomplish both goals?

Time is always an issue. I ask Millie whether the faculty has considered asking students to grade pieces holistically in a group as the faculty does. She acknowledges the value of students' setting the standards for their work and developing the criteria in concert with peers, but she says, "Students might like to look at work and grade it holistically, but we ask them to use their class time differently. Besides, students spend a lot of time developing rubrics for their exhibitions."

Grades matter to Millie not at all. She explains her own assessment methods, which are much more humane than an arbitrary measure delivered from a distance. Millie depends on a personal relationship with the students she grades, not on a standard for all. "I assess as we go along. When I look at students' daily work, I ask myself whether the work shows they understand. I put check marks and we talk. If I'm not sure, then the student and I have a conversation the next day, and I tease out whether they understand. I don't grade that daily work until I am convinced the student understands. I continuously review kids' work to determine whether students can restate the problem and describe the process." Millie acknowledges that what pulls down a grade is undone work and she is tough about maintaining an explicit standard: "When it comes to grading portfolios, I average the grades on the individual pieces and I look at the number of assignments completed. Kids get a zero for pieces they don't have ready."

At the end of each term, Millie will ask students to fill out a two-page form, "Reflections on IMP and Me," to capture the growth and understanding that she knows the portfolios contain. Students answer questions she poses: "What have I learned this term? This is how I learned it. . . . This is what I'd do differently. . . . This is what I'd like more of. . . . This is what I need from our class. . . . This is what I want to contribute to our class. . . . I want to add my thoughts/feelings about this. . . . And I believe that my grade should be _____." She either agrees or disagrees with their assessment. Students can contest the grade she gives them in a form that has at the bottom:

> In Fenway, a grade is only one measurement of a student's learning, but an important one. If you disagree with any of my comments here, please see me *immediately after class* to set up a conference where we can discuss our differences. If I do not hear from you I will assume that you accept my conclusions as fair.

In Millie's experience, students often grade themselves higher than she does, and if they are dissatisfied, they can revisit their portfolios anytime and redo their work, and often choose to do this during class time.

Millie recognizes the tension between standards for all and the development of individual students' understanding. She has resolved the dilemma—at least for the time being—by the following actions: She keeps her eye on student learning as exemplified by the growth she sees in their actual work; she eschews daily grades and assesses by a uniform measure only at the end of the term; and she insists on completed work and holds students to that clear, concrete standard. The story could end here. But such a mechanical list easily covers up the real problems.

Tug-of-War, Again

The tug-of-war between personal growth and standards of knowledge surfaces yet again in the math portfolios. Millie is well aware that "students have poor work habits. They have never been expected to perform; they come from schools where expectations are low. I need to see a change in work habits. It gets in my way if there is none." She immediately zeroes in on Mikell Jones, who has, she laments, poor work habits. All he did in his old school was play basketball. His mother put him in Fenway. "No matter what we do at Fenway, he still hasn't bought into school. He can't establish work habits and there is a pattern. I can see it in his portfolio."

During math I saw Mikell blatantly copying a friend's work. He says, "It keeps me from being down in school," by which he means behind. "School takes up a lot of time." Millie is distressed about Mikell and others like him. She knows the indicators of success are "buying into school" and improved work habits, and Mikell isn't there yet. But she feels the tension between individuals like Mikell and a standard operating procedure. She says over and over again in every symbolic and real way: "We work on deadlines. We have to. We need kids to succeed in real-world performances, not just get good grades. We need to look at their products and ask did the kid perform well? We have to set policy for everyone, but we have to make room for the kids who don't fit the mold." There is no escaping the inconsistency here, but this bind is an occupational hazard for teachers who care about students in Mikell's situation, another example of Fenway's tug-of-war with itself. Push Mikell too hard and he will drop out of school, and where will that get Millie or Mikell?

Millie believes adamantly that Fenway should add specific academic goals to its mission statement: "Even if kids can't demonstrate that they are meeting those goals, the school needs them out there for kids to see. It's about striving." What happens when you say that out loud, I ask. "Nothing, absolutely nothing. I've been saying it for years" (see Delpit, 1993).

Balancing Portfolios and Exhibitions

Fenway's portfolios have always competed with Coalition-style exhibitions. The faculty still struggles to find the right balance between portfolios, which require considerable written evidence plus diligent completion of all the work, and exhibitions, where students display their knowledge publicly. Both forms of assessment are evolving at Fenway.

It was a "major breakthrough" when faculty realized how students could use portfolios—at that time a collection of assigned work—in an exhibition format to demonstrate what they knew in front of peers and adults. The administration and faculty have defined exhibitions of student knowledge as a performance of skills, and demonstrations as explaining the contents of portfolios (Southworth, 1992). In these "Demonstrations of Portfolios," students talk about their completed work in front of an audience. This distinction between exhibitions and portfolios still holds, but the goal is an organic relationship between the two methods. Right now, however, it is the more public exhibitions that push teachers systematically to think through the standards as a group. Millie points out a possible reason: schemes—or rubrics, as they are usually called—for scoring exhibitions are created in each class through discussion with students, but portfolios are still graded by the teacher with a letter grade each term. Exhibitions are not graded, but students make up the exhibition score sheets, which include the evaluative categories of inadequate, satisfactory/competent, or exceptional. "Kids know what those terms mean because *they* have been part of the standards-setting discussion." This process of developing rubrics is an important one for teachers and students to go through together. Exhibitions are meant to show what students can do, and scores help students to know when and how to redo parts of their exhibitions.

The exhibitions have evolved sufficiently that Fenway now invites outside judges from nearby colleges and the community to score them, which involves heavy scheduling. Millie characteristically sees these judged exhibitions from the students' perspective. She champions the individual's need to be ready and fights for students to have sufficient preparation time: "We in the math department are getting away from a rigid schedule of telling kids when they have to exhibit before judges. In our department we are not making a schedule around when we say students are ready, but giving kids a chance to say when *they* are ready. The administrative leader of the math team wants exhibitions done this term, but I stood up for kids who would not be successful because they are not ready."

Portfolios and exhibitions intersect in other ways that go beneath the surface of mechanical teaching strategies. In order to prepare for major exhibitions, students do an optional short (under five minutes) presentation of a piece of their portfolio work that counts for 25% of their term grade. Their actual portfolio counts for 25%. If students choose not to do a presentation, their portfolio counts as 50% of their term grade. I saw one presentation during my visit. A poised ninth grader with an inviting smile put her performing all into demonstrating patterns she noticed in counting how many different squares there are on a checkerboard. In her baggy pants, oversized flannel work shirt, clunky shoes, pulled-back hair, and small gold earrings, Gina is a picture from a teen fashion magazine. It's a "dynamite" presentation, says an unofficial outsider, but we agree that the mathematical ideas aren't there. In what is probably her first public effort of the year and her first high school presentation, she is energetic as she counts the different sized squares on the teacher-drawn diagram on the board, but in this five minutes she makes no leap from this example to the mathematical generalizations that IMP has built into the lesson. The class might have helped her to go deeper, but none of her 18 peers ask questions that might probe her thinking. (I was mindful of Marlon's caution that for students to ask questions the "air" has to be right. The tone in the room seemed fine to me.) The teacher does not probe either. The grade is C+.

As Fenway teachers struggle to set academic expectations and face the distinctions between warm, supportive assessments and cool analytic appraisals (McDonald, 1992), they have to fight the tendency to give good grades too easily (Southworth, 1992). A faculty member points out that a presentation like Gina's represents progress: "We want kids to look alert and not say Huh? when they don't know." By that standard, Gina is an A+ at looking alert, but Fenway has passed the point of rewarding students with good grades for superficial alertness. Alertness must include self-awareness that mathematical knowledge is lacking, an internal trigger to push the student toward asking for help. Gina has not met that standard nor has she been given a clue as to how she might proceed. The grade—accurate as it probably is—has become the central focus rather than the mathematical learning. This five-minute presentation is a microcosm of the shifting ground between the old conceptions of learning in high school and the new. How to get students to use their minds well, to think rather than memorize, to utilize well performance-based assessments to promote learning, are all encapsulated in the questions raised by Gina's presentation. Millie's sparring partner over the Coalition chart, Janet Hamilton, is a grade above Gina and still wants to be given math examples to practice at her seat; students and teachers know how to do that. But the new ways of teaching and learning are not yet perfected to the same degree and neither students nor teachers have all the rough edges smoothed out. Nor does anyone tend to consider how much time it takes to make this shift after the years and years of doing it the old way.

Some Fenway faculty believe that these presentations and the exhibitions they lead to are a waste of time for the students who are not exhibiting. Gina's peers are more obviously engaged with Gina than they are with the math. A male with similar near-combat boots asks her as she sits down, "How much did you pay for those?" which might confirm that point of view. But others recognize that developing a participating audience is how Fenway builds an academic community and believe that if teachers model an attitude of high expectations on the part of the exhibitor and the onlookers, then students will rise to them. This debate does not interest Millie; she has a different agenda. She wants her students to finish their portfolios. She won't necessarily have them do exhibitions for judges in February when other departments do them. First and foremost, "Kids have to be ready," she says emphatically.

Ultimately, students have a Senior Exit Interview, as the Senior Exit Portfolios are sometimes called, and this includes several portfolio items from each subject discipline. The exit interviews are retained in the official files like a transcript, and include a longer and longer list of requirements each year as the school gets more savvy about the possibilities. Fenway's math goal for the Senior Exit Interview is to include a math position paper, a math model, and representation or argument about a mathematical idea. Since the exit interviews grow out of the portfolios, which are now in their infancy, it is thought that it will take some time before that goal is realized, but having such a goal helps clarify the role of portfolios as they support exhibitions and exit interviews.

One theme that comes clear about portfolios and exhibitions at Fenway is the multifaceted need for time measured in different frames. Not only do teachers and students need more time—measured in class periods—to set standards together so that portfolios are no longer graded by adults, but they need time—measured in weeks—for Millie's students' to develop sufficiently so they can "be ready" for their exhibitions. They need time—measured in years—to sufficiently develop portfolios so that the exit interviews will be complex, rich, and full, and time—measured in many years—for students and teachers to knowingly appreciate the new ways of teaching and learning. These varying time frames work against standards imposed by any system on individual teaching and students.

A Weekly Math Team Meeting: Pursuing Large Purposes

The regular math team weekly meeting, I am told, is rarely canceled. Staff members look forward to it, learn from it, and depend on it to anchor their classroom work. Today an emergency union meeting conflicts, but that does not stop the math team. The math team goes to the meeting, but leaves after five minutes to keep their regular schedule, even as potential political and personal consequences hang over the union gathering (the air in that room is indeed crackling).

Four teachers form the core team, along with Linda Nathan, the acting director who is mainly on child-care leave but returns each week to facilitate the meetings. I am present in my role as Four Seasons documentor along with an evaluator for IMP and a math consultant from TERC.

The plan is to look at two pieces of student work and grade them holistically. Abby Schirmer turns to me and says, "Are you desperate to see some holistic grading?" I am but I deny it. She explains that she feels an urgency to talk about an unintended consequence of the term portfolio deadline: Students are cheating on their portfolios. She continues, "Suddenly, the week has gotten out of control. Not an occasional kid, but many kids are copying work to finish their portfolios. Up till now kids cooperated and shared and helped each other, but yesterday a kid accused me of losing her folder and I don't think she'd done any work."

The discussion takes off. The pace is intense, and bespeaks a group that knows each other well and likes to be together. They move fast between small examples and large purposes. A quick exchange with Paul Harrison about the mechanics of practice produces the following surprise:

ABBY: The copying happens when I give kids back their work.
PAUL: You hand kids work back with grades?
ABBY: Don't you?
PAUL: No. I keep it in a locked file after it has a grade on it.

But the underlying issue is ever-present: "The biggest piece is not the individual incident of cheating, but what kind of a culture are we promoting here." Millie asks which kids are cheating. "Are they not doing any day-to-day work? Or don't they have enough time to do it all, even though they try?" Teachers think through the issues: If the math activities have so many different solutions, then no paper should look like any other paper, right? Someone muses that if you can "steal" another paper, maybe the curriculum is too standardized. Maybe we need to have more open-endedness. Teachers mention the humanities poster assignments, due today. Kids have prepared, among other things, a campaign for or against legalizing marijuana, which has provoked much excited talk in the halls: "Let me see yours'" and "You better do a good job or you'll get graded down" and "Please help me draw." Faculty agree that students couldn't steal each others' posters. (Millie later mentions gently that even posters had a standardized quality; kids could have been asked to demonstrate their campaigns in more ways than in a poster.)

Two threads run through the discussion. The math consultant from TERC believes that Fenway's culture embeds the problem: "This cheating is a symptom of kids wanting to do the least amount of work. The ethic is how to outsmart teachers and get by with the minimum. So cheating is often the best solution." Others, including Millie, believe that there are more ways to interpret "cheating" than students' attempt to get work done with the least amount of effort. They believe that when students care enough to copy work, caring ratchets up the value they place on school demands. If students didn't care, they would just opt out, which is not to say they would drop out, but they would just not turn in any work.

Standards of knowing come up in relation to why cheating doesn't help students in the Fenway system. Math assessments go beyond the portfolio, and even the portfolio is but a small part of the grade. The TERC consultant points out: "If you have to know more than is required in the portfolio, you can cheat and it won't help you down the road." Linda gets inside a student's head: "If I copied my work from you, and I still have to stand up before peers in an exhibition, it will be obvious what I don't understand." This leads to a discussion (perhaps an example of how exhibitions overshadow portfolios) of how to engender exhibitions with more variety so students won't be exhibiting the same problems.

The talk veers off for a moment to nationwide cheating and Millie brings it back to the problem at hand: " Maybe what students are doing isn't cheating; maybe we have put unrealistic pressure on them to finish. After all, they have considerably less time than a California term. Maybe kids who are behind should be able to negotiate undone work or get incompletes." The faculty agrees. They move the deadline to give kids another week, even as they are mindful of vacillating between strict real-world deadlines and the real students in their charge. Linda says, "Now let's play this out. Would

I give Mikell Jones an extra week before I fail him? Otherwise, we never have a deadline and we're back to where we always are."

Perhaps thinking about Mikell reminds Millie of her commitment to making success possible for students. Though I have heard her say several times that she looks for every way to keep students from failing, she slips in her thought here as if it were new: "It just dawned on me that I never mention the word failure with portfolios; portfolios are about where students are now." Whether Mikell is in her mind or not, this comment serves to remind the rest that students like Mikell need an extra week and calling him on his failure to meet the current deadline will not serve him well in the long term.

While she has the floor, Millie retells yesterday's exchange over the Coalition principles with Janet Hamilton, and reminds her colleagues how students think: "Kids haven't yet made the transition; we're asking them to make enormous changes."

The group turns to a scheduling discussion meant to inform each other of their whereabouts and activities for the next month. Within two or three weeks the team will: meet with the rest of the faculty to talk about whether Fenway should apply to become a charter school under new state regulations, go for more IMP math training in New Haven, attend another evening meeting for parents (Linda tosses out an aside here: "Millie and Paul, you did a terrific job explaining IMP to parents last week"), and attend a night community service awards assembly and a nighttime Hispanic Heritage Month celebration. As representatives of the Coalition, Paul will consult with teachers in Cleveland and Millie with teachers in Louisville. Linda asks what they would like for dinner at their evening faculty meeting, and volunteers to take their children to the Children's Museum when schools are closed for Veteran's Day and the teachers go to IMP training in New Haven. Linda's supportive concern for their welfare is a clue to the faculty's willingness to work incredibly hard. Morale is high; the climate is one of mutual support.

The last item is the cover letter to go with the narrative report cards to parents. Paul, another Four Seasons team member, is in charge, but he is finding it hard. He says what I have heard in each site visit: "I'm having trouble because I don't like doing it alone. I need to do it in a group." Someone quickly dictates a possible draft and the meeting is over.

This meeting, one site of the tug-of-war between personal growth and academic achievement, is the place where faculty build community and culture. The discussion began with a concern about cheating, but really explores the efficacy of Fenway's current portfolios. The faculty talk is a crucible for working out values, which are not dichotomized as either/or, as a tug-of-war might suggest. Rather, faculty members are joining together as they work out their own responses to the hard assessment questions, even as they regularly change sides of the rope.

Portfolios Only Connect

The stakes are not just assessment. Between my visit and writing this account, a Fenway student allegedly shot someone in his neighborhood and will, if convicted, serve a long prison term. Fenway's highly permeable boundary between the lives of students in and out of school requires, as Maxine Greene (1993) puts it in "Diversity and Inclusion: Toward a Curriculum for Human Beings," "a confronting of the contradictions, the instances of savagery, the neglect, and the possibility of care" (p. 220). The Fenway faculty are fully engaged in that struggle through face-to-face participation in a trusted group. Their emerging values engender standards, not standards set in stone or measured against universal compliance, but standards of caring. Framed this way, assessment is but a small part of the Fenway mission.

Portfolios only connect. The book *Only Connect: Readings on Children's Literature* (Travers, 1969) sits at eye level on my bookshelf, and its title flashed into my head as I visited three schools where I worked my schedule around observing collegial talk. In looking again into the origins of the phrase, I found this evocative passage in a P. L. Travers essay

> When I was at Radcliffe last year students used to crowd into my small apartment once a week and the talk was so good, they were all so alive, so open to ideas, and so ready to fight me for them. I liked that. And I remember that on one occasion I said—and it still seems to me true—that thinking was linking. At that, one marvelous girl blazed out at me, "Yes! Only connect!"
>
> "Only connect" was the exact phrase I had been leading up to and it has been precious to me ever since I read *Howards End,* of which it is the epigraph. Perhaps, indeed, it's the theme of all Forster's writing, the attempt to link a passionate scepticism with the desire for meaning, to find the human key to the inhuman world about us; to connect the individual with the community, the known with the unknown; to relate the past to the present and both to the future. (p. 183)

That philosophical weight is a lot to carry in mathematics portfolios, and I don't mean to overload them with unnecessary baggage. Rather, any topic that is rich in possibility for grappling with honest human concerns in a safe setting will spark the same electric talk. Teachers here talk about cheating and open up possibilities for a changed definition—that embedded in cheating is the possibility for increased caring, indicative of an increased interest in academic success rather than a school sin. In an altered definition cheating would no longer be something to get away with, but rather another element of peers' using each other as resources. The faculty considers the possibility that the locus of the copying problem is not in the student: that the same math problems for everyone, even when they are open-ended, do not provide enough entry points, and result in students' copying from each other. They consider the possibility that if students are not genuinely engaged in the work, copying is an easy out for them. They take responsibility for making an effort to entice the students who are reluctant participants by offering a chance for negotiation and compromise. The discussion tracks back to the tug-of-war about whether the standard school conventions—timeliness and individual effort—are worth salvaging. They ask if the problem resides in the curriculum: Is it too standardized? too mechanical in its deadlines? too thoughtless about individuals? Or is the problem adults mistrusting students? Millie's confidence that students can do the work (even if they might choose not to) prevails. She reminds the group that portfolios are not about failure, but about where students are now. This moral and epistemological conversation goes well beyond the issues represented by collections of student work. Such conversation depends, if it is to be sufficiently generative, on leadership, colleagueship, shared commitment to students, and what P. L. Travers has identified as the talk that links thought. The Fenway math meeting has those attributes.

SCHOOL REFORM BEYOND FENWAY

Fenway's Process as a Model

The arduous work of school change can be exhilarating. Since practice mandated from outside the classroom no longer serves schools, the absence of a "right" way allows educators the opportunity to create answers for themselves. Especially at the high school level, where traditional disciplinary knowledge reigns, no quick and easy answers exist as teachers pioneer new ways to rethink teaching and learning. Millie's search for success vivifies the confusing stumbles and the clear heights that all changing schools encounter on the path toward reform.

Fenway may be in the forefront of school reform issues, but its goal is not the edification or revitalization of Boston's school system. Fenway's founding director Larry Myatt (on a year's leave as Coalition Fellow at Brown) does not see the school as a model; he does not think official Boston does either: "In 10 years we have had scads of visitors from far away, but only once did the Boston school system sanction a visit." According to him, "No one is pressing on us. Fenway is light years ahead of anyone else, but we are not in this to convince 50 other school systems to do what we do.

We just like to do it." I suspect that in spite of itself Fenway will contribute to the larger school reform conversation. Boston school officials may not be watching, but Fenway's central place in the national reform networks assures interested spectators. Since school change is a process with infinite alternative paths, the more models in existence, the better for everyone.

Over the years, this regularly assigned faculty, once part of the larger and more impersonal English High, have had extraordinary professional-development opportunities. What small, energetic, thoughtful faculties with good leadership and opportunities for their own growth can do to push forward on the (so far) intractable problems in urban schools is yet to be seen. Working out ambivalence, confronting contradictions, and rethinking schooling is the challenge. "Yield: Cultures Crossing" is a sign of the times both at Fenway and beyond.

Engagement as Accountability

Millie is right in the middle, connecting students with each other, reminding faculty how the world looks through students' eyes, acting as a conduit for network-created knowledge, fighting for tough explicit expectations at the same time she is making room for individuals and demonstrating to skeptical adults that every child can succeed. Millie brings her personal values to the school community, and through interaction with the values of others, the community grows stronger. For Millie, being tough and trusting students are not incompatible; her stance is emblematic of the moral tug-of-war the faculty enacts. Her engagement in this tug-of-war is what makes her trustworthy and accountable. As parents and the public begin to encounter more teachers who are deeply engaged in figuring out the complexities of teaching and learning, they will see how an increase in teachers' knowledge and professional capacity improves schools for students. Teachers like Millie can and should be trusted by parents and the wider public to make decisions about their teaching and students' learning both because they are skilled professionals and because they work in settings that continue to foster their development.

Fenway's school reform effort is a decade old, but its intensive focus on assessment, especially portfolio development, is essentially new. Millie and her faculty do not yet have firm answers to the questions they raise, even as they go forward each day; the mode is exploration of possibilities while they are in motion. But the questions practitioners ask in the course of a school day have a more concrete sense. What to do with Mikell Jones and others like him who have not yet "bought into school" is an urgent quandary. Should we give him an extra week to finish his portfolio or will that defeat our purpose in teaching him that lateness has consequences? Or does a firm deadline he can't meet just confirm for him that he does not belong in this place where academic conventions rule? No matter how hard we try to teach the codes necessary for success, he still copies his work from a friend because "school takes up a lot of time." Millie's solutions—make room for students who don't fit the mold, keep the word failure out of his life, and give him a zero for undone work—are inconsistent, but practical. Millie struggles, wavers, and changes her mind as do others who care deeply about the Mikells of this world. She keeps her eyes on the child as she and her colleagues courageously keep picking through the philosophical, moral, and practical decisions that make teaching intellectually engaging and personally rewarding.

CODA

Making practice visible, as these teachers have done with their colleagues, does not mean making it measurable. Not all learning leaves evidence in a folder, nor are the complexities of thinking easily quantifiable (Carini, 1991). If standardized tests narrowed curriculum over many decades, then it may take an equal number of years to broaden the curriculum and enlarge the ways students represent their learning in portfolios. As for the vise that whomps children—portfolios are better than testing, but more change is needed. The portfolios don't yet totally honor the complex developmental path of children.

Guardians of the political and pedagogical process must be vigilant so that ubiquitously similar portfolios do not become another way to make conformity visible or to exclude children from the right to a quality education. This perch requires double vision. Assessment politics require keeping a steady eye on the children and their daily learning, but also on large purposes. As Vito Perrone (1991) says, "To lose a focus on democracy—for example, not to be closely connected in our practice to the world, its problems, and its promise—is to lose the moral base of our work" (p. 9).

AFTERWORD

On Standards and Teaching

It will have occurred to most readers of this book that it is a book about portfolios in the same way that *Howard's End* is a novel about an estate, or Hamlet a play about a kingdom. Like these other works, this one—in the domain of teaching and learning in schools—is really about the pesky trouble we have whenever we try in the most important matters to reconcile head and heart. In other words, it is about standards—and of how one may at once hold them high and avoid being hanged by them.

In her own recent work on the same subject, Dennie Palmer Wolf (1994) takes the reader on a tour of the medieval cathedral of Modena. On one wall, cut into the stone, the author notes for our benefit the grooves and half-spheres that once served as common measures for the medieval Modena market—this much cloth, that much grain. On another wall, she notes the deliberate imposition of a much later era: a mosaic of photographic bits commemorating the Modena people who died struggling against fascism. From the juxtaposition, Wolf conjures up an elegant distinction:

> The grooves and the *partizans* are two distinct faces of what we mean when we speak of standards. The grooves are stable, civic inventions of the first order: reliable tools that work across different goods, buyers, days, and times. Like the kilogram, the teaspoon, or the footcandle, they are international, declarative, and firm. . . .
>
> But the photographs under glass are an equally necessary kind of standard . . . [raising] the question, "But what is worth measuring?" Because they are nominations of what is best, or brave, or worth following, such standards work by provoking allegiance, resistance, conversation, even debate. (pp. 86–87)

Part of the trouble we have when we speak about standards—at least outside Modena—is that the different meanings we intuitively attach to the concept don't stay put on one wall or the other. In teaching, they get all mixed up within the wild triangle defined by us, the students, and the things we try to teach them. This doesn't make the different meanings any less distinct than in Modena, however—nor the paradox of how to manage them any less difficult.

Kathe Jervis offers us the Modena paradox in three unexpectedly similar American places: two at either end of the cross-continental Interstate 90, in Bellevue and Boston, the other a couple of hours further east by boat or car, in Provincetown. In these places, some extraordinary teachers try daily to negotiate the paradox. Kathe invites us into their professional lives. We find ourselves eager to accept the invitation, because we sense immediately that each teacher is wrestling with the questions that are at the heart of school reform everywhere today: What are standards anyway? Are they more like the grooves or the partisans? Shall we think about them as codified, abstract, and fixed civic inventions; or as intuitive, provocative, developmental guideposts? Whatever they are, where do they come from? The head or the heart? In searching for them, shall we foreground the world or the child?

By answering the last of these questions so resolutely—by telling us throughout her "portfolio stories" to keep our eyes on the child—the author helps us tolerate continuing ambiguity with regard to all the other questions. In effect, she solves the paradox, and in the way one must solve any paradox—by dissolving it. It turns out that the children, when viewed up close rather than as some distant object of policymaking, are unmistakably in the world and the world in them. In viewing the child up close, one inescapably uses both head and heart. "Only connect," E. M. Forster said, and Kathe reminds us. In teaching, this means struggling to read the actual Greg, Grace, and Mikell—the children of Provincetown, Bellevue, and Boston—as players in a world that makes demands on them. And it means taking them seriously with all their complex strengths and needs, even as one takes the demands seriously. As Kathe's "portfolio stories" reveal, this connected knowing does not make teachers any more certain of how to act toward the children than they otherwise would be—whether at any moment to hang back or push, hold back or graduate. But, without eyes on the child—and the world in the child—one cannot make such difficult decisions wisely, and might as well be teaching or evaluating by remote control.

Though it may seem to some readers an extreme analogy, I find it useful to compare the dilemma that Kathe explores in this book—between "the Scylla and Charybdis of children's natural development and school-based expectations"—to the dilemma doctors experience treating a terminally ill patient in a high-tech hospital. The doctor cannot simply take the purely "developmental" route—to wait for death—since death may not come without a doctor's act of omission. Nor can doctors depend utterly on the rulebook—best practice as defined by law, ethics, expert medical opinion, and the hospital's governing board. They must take both these things into account, but as they are reflected in the actual patient. They must strive to understand the rules by what they see in the patient, and to know the development of death for what it looks like and feels like there.

Such an attitude of attention and caring softens the points of an otherwise impossibly hard dilemma. And it is the same in teaching. That is why Millie Sanders, pondering the continuous struggle at Fenway between honoring public standards and respecting the developmental pace of students, "immediately zeroes in on Mikell Jones." Public standards are mere abstractions except as they relate to the realities and prospects of actual people like Mikell Jones—who "isn't there yet," but by whose light Millie can better see where "there" is and of how Mikell might be helped to strive for it. Marla English and Barb Renfrow-Baker negotiate the same dilemma at an earlier crucial junction, striving to create enough slack so that some of their children can come to literacy "later than the system permits," and to ensure that others, like Tim, are not written off by the system. They accomplish both not by discounting the system's Student Learning Objectives, but by turning them into "entry slips"—footnotes to the child. The main business of their teaching is Tim himself, and Josette, Matthew, Suki, and Grace. But the footnotes matter too. Marla likes the "dissonance" they create across the whole text of her teaching.

In Provincetown, the standards dilemma seems less salient, but that is an illusion—artifact of a beneficial policy vacuum at the time of Kathe's visit to Provincetown. At that time, no one "higher up" in the system had yet installed the curriculum frameworks and framework-based assessments now aiming to direct teaching and learning in Provincetown and the rest of Massachusetts. Luckily, Provincetown has the ballast to accommodate these new winds blowing. It took years to store it up, and this storing up is the subtext of Kathe's Provincetown chapter. Remember that the efforts she discovered underway there had a four-year history by the time of her visit. Such policy initiatives as the one in Massachusetts cannot possibly succeed without the kind of worrying about standards, the searching for them in the real work of actual children, that Kathe recounts in all her stories. One cannot command such attitudes to appear. They can only be the product of a slow storing up. On the other hand, one can design policies that aid the storing up.

A PRACTICAL GUIDE

In using storytelling to deal with what I called above the pesky business of standards, Kathe lets the medium bear part of the message. The idiosyncrasies of stories, and also their tendency to catch us up in their drift, are also qualities of schools—and exactly the ones that disable top-down policymaking. And there is no doubt that this book takes a subtle swat at top-down policymaking. Yet one can also read across stories when they are set side by side. Reading across Kathe's stories, one finds a practical guide to child-focused and standards-based teaching, a guide that can serve policy as well as practice. It is a guide that dissolves the Modena paradox.

I have already highlighted above three of the most important pieces of advice in this guide: that the growth process takes time, that it cannot be commanded from above, and that its core strategy involves keeping one's eyes on the child. There is one other very important piece of advice here: Even if a school follows the other advice—manages to find enough time to grow, gets somehow clear of top-down mandates (for example, by becoming a charter school—as one of the schools Kathe writes about has done), and tries to focus all eyes on the child—this will not be enough. That is because really seeing children, and seeing in them the real demands of the world and the children's power to meet those demands, also requires depth of field.

Nearly everywhere—certainly in Provincetown, Bellevue, and Boston—the working conditions of teaching are such that teachers are not spontaneously inclined to keep their eyes on the child—at least not in the way that Kathe means. True, they are compelled to keep their eyes on the children, but the plural makes an important difference. Teachers must monitor the group, make sure that the collective experience stays apparently engaging, productive, and safe. Under these circumstances, they become accustomed to making quick judgments about the child as member of the group: He's paying attention now, she's about to cause trouble again, he's lost, she's quick, and so on. But to see the child as the child really is takes a special effort. This effort is less about stepping closer than it is about stepping back—as I say, gaining depth of field.

How does one gain depth of field in seeing children—particularly given the fast flow of school life, and the ordinary scarcity of opportunities to step back? Reading across Kathe's stories, one can infer a very good answer to this question. The schools described in this book use four tools to help them step back to see their children in greater depth of field. As you will see in the following list, they are designed to work together.

THEORY

The teachers whose work is described in this book decided to take up the work for a number of personal reasons—some of which Kathe names—and also for one important reason that is less personal: Each had encountered at least one theory that suggested they should, and the theory made sense to them. That is why the names of theorists are sprinkled across the stories: John Dewey, Pat Carini, Donald Graves, Ted Sizer, Howard Gardner, and so on. This is not to say that good teachers depend on theorists to tell them what to do. But a good idea or two—supplied from the outside, but with respect for the complexities of the inside—can help a good teacher stand back from these complexities and reflect on them.

The portfolio work in Provincetown began, Kathe explains, "when several Veterans Memorial Elementary School faculty heard Howard Gardner and came away intrigued." The attraction they felt to Gardner's ideas was, of course, a product of their own preparation and willingness to acquire a different perspective on their work. But the ideas themselves were crucial too.

It was the same thing in Bellevue: Marla English and Barb Renfrow-Baker were deeply affected by their first Foxfire encounter in 1991 because they were ready to rethink their practice. "After we took the Foxfire course," Barb explains, "we put more decisions in the children's hands. When the block building area grew so big that it infringed on the class meeting area, we put the problem to the children." Later, in trying to implement the district's new standards, they took the next logical step of making that the children's problem too. But this is a logical step only within a context that has been affected by the ideas of Dewey and Wigginton. In fact, within the dominant culture of teaching—and, indeed, of policymaking—teachers who make children responsible for their learning are seen as shirking their own responsibility. That's why so many teachers stand around feeling useless and guilty when their students are hard at work in cooperative learning teams or in other self-directed activities.

And, in the Fenway story, there is the account of the difference that the simplest contact with a theorist's ideas made in Millie Sanders's self-confidence and reputation. She heard a presentation on portfolios by Giselle Martin-Kniep, and came back to school excited to share what she'd learned. A colleague recalls the moment: "The day she whipped out a definition of portfolios and said with real passion, 'See, it's not about the teacher deciding. It is the interaction about the work between the student and the teacher,' she became our 'portfolio expert.'" It is fashionable now to decry the one-shot professional development presentation, and, indeed, its association with the "in-servicing" of teachers justifies the skepticism. But this anecdote reminds us of the power of a good idea—even when presented without reference to particular contexts—if it manages to connect with a self-directed teacher, and if that teacher happens to work in a ripe context.

NETWORKS

The teachers Kathe describes in this book are lucky to get their good ideas not only from presentations and reading, but also from networks of reform-minded colleagues. Recall, first of all, that they are all part of a network of teachers called the Four Seasons Project, that they know each other—and Kathe—as a result of this association, though they work in different communities and even on different coasts. Moreover, as a result of this network, they share an electronic mail and conferencing system, so they can keep current with each other's work. The Four Seasons Project, founded by the National Center for Restructuring Education, Schools, and Teaching at Teachers College, Columbia University, is based on ideas. Among them is the idea that performance assessment can be a powerful tool for teaching well, if it honors differences in the child and is not simply imposed on practice by policy. Indeed, the network was formed precisely to raise a teacher's voice against the mindless imposition of policy in the area of assessment—an objective well met in this book

Meanwhile, the Four Seasons Project is composed of members of three other networks that are also idea-based and activist: Foxfire, Project Zero, and the Coalition of Essential Schools. In effect, because it is a report from a network of networks, this book is more powerful than it would be if it were merely another set of case studies of reforming practice. That is because it will be used within these networks to push on from here. More people will visit the schools it describes. They'll get in touch with Cathy, Barb, Marla, and Millie through e-mail, invite them to regional network conferences, use their stories as touchstones in their efforts to change their own schools or to affect their own district or state policies. That is how reform networks work; they encourage collective wisdom to grow, and cultivate collective strength to keep it growing. One cannot underestimate their power in this regard. Getting over current failings in the way we teach American children—our habits of sorting them into winners and losers, of reducing their work thoughtlessly to tokens like grades and test scores, of failing to see them as the people they really are and can become—will be every bit as challenging on the social level as efforts on the personal level to get over obesity or drug dependence. Just as the individual person cannot manage the latter challenges alone, neither can the individual school manage the former challenges alone. In both cases, it takes networked strength and courage to step back from the ordinary running on of life—to put things in perspective, as they say—or, as I say above, to gain depth of field.

RITUAL

Among the things that networks trade in, perhaps the most important is the rituals they invent or scrounge. Three rituals are prominent in the stories of this book: the Collaborative Assessment Conference ritual in Provincetown, the Descriptive Review ritual in Bellevue, and the Tuesday portfolio meeting ritual at Fenway. The purpose of all of them is to structure seeing and the conversation about what is seen such that different perspectives are acknowledged and shared. Of course, school is ordinarily full of rituals, but most are designed to suggest convergence rather than to explore divergence: the faculty meeting ritual full of announcements with no discussion, the lunchroom conversation ritual that avoids any mention of students, the parent-teacher conference ritual that is all one-way communication, and so on. But the convergence such rituals suggest is a cover-up—of disagreements in the faculty, of teachers' worries about particular children, of teachers' uncertainties about the real progress their students are making. The rituals that Kathe highlights in this book are deliberately countercultural in that they not only admit difference, but try to put it to work to benefit children.

The rituals also cut across the grain of ordinary discourse and ordinary habits of interaction. For example, both the Collaborative Assessment Conference and the Descriptive Review artificially separate description from judgment. The artifice is powerful in that it illuminates for participants the ways in which the ordinary mix of description and judgment compromises genuine seeing. In this and other respects, these rituals are strict. In the CAC, colleagues must look at the student work in silence, and then proceed through a set of prescribed questions. In the Descriptive Review, the opening presentation follows a specified series of perspectives on the child—physical gesture, temperament, relationships, formal academics, and interests—and may not be interrupted. Then it proceeds through formal rounds of turn-taking questions. Again, the artifice is powerful inasmuch as it releases participants from their habits and compels seeing.

Anyone who has ever participated in a group scoring ritual knows how powerful—and extraordinary in terms of ordinary school meetings—the Tuesday portfolio meetings at Fenway must be. Describing them, Millie says, "We sit together each Tuesday to look at work in portfolios. We all look at a piece of work and give it a score from 1 to 5 and then compare our responses and discuss the differences. Then, based on discussion, we negotiate a score. We have to convince others of our thinking. It's a slow process. Then when we assess students on our own, we can tell how far off we are from the group". Even in this era of experimentation with performance assessment, the simple series of acts that Millie describes here are extraordinarily rare in school life. Teachers ordinarily do not discuss their judgments of student work with each other. Though they negotiate all the time with their students, they almost never negotiate with each other. And they are almost never called on to convince anyone of anything—except the principal occasionally, and then most commonly in the rhetoric of a paternalistic organization. But, as Millie and Kathe make clear, these nearly absent habits of interaction are crucial to the development of a culture of standards in school—at least one that honors the Modena paradox.

TEXTMAKING

During the first year of the portfolio experiments in Provincetown, a ritual was established in which teachers and visiting Project Zero staff retired at the end of the school day to a local restaurant, Napi's, in order "to hash out the philosophy and mechanics of portfolios." During these meetings, as Kathe reports, "the Project Zero staff took notes which they circulated back to the faculty." This is a good example of what I mean by textmaking—the effort to put on paper, or in some other textual format (a videotape, an audiotape), the complications of one's thinking, doing, or feeling. Textmaking is a crucial tool for gaining the necessary depth of field for really seeing children, because it stops what is otherwise fleeting, crystallizes it, and thus renders it consultable later. The Provincetown teachers may have depended initially on Project Zero to be their textmakers, but they also got into the habit themselves. The *Portfolio Handbook* (Provincetown Faculty, 1991) they devised is, in effect, an extension of their Napi's notes. It enabled them to keep track of what was a very long and tortuous developmental process, gave them the record of what they thought about last month so that they could revise it this month, lent them the opportunity—otherwise so rare in school—to move past the informal and superficial consensus that masks real faultlines of disagreement, to on-the-page-at-least-for-now consensus. The latter is the kind that can make for progress because it tells you where you really are at any point, whereas the former gets you into lots of trouble because it continuously misleads you as to where you all are.

Marla's class handbook in Bellevue is another good example of textmaking. Here the point is not only to explain things to oneself and perhaps serve as a text within which one works out mutual understandings with one's teaching partner, but also to provide an "entry point" for still others—like the parents, student teachers, and volunteers Marla and Barb recruit.

But texts need not be written ones. "Fenway lives by stories," Kathe tells us, by which she means that the school's standards of practice are made manifest, continually examined and critiqued, and passed on to others by means of an oral storytelling culture. Whether written or oral, texts enable teachers to get a grip on their own experience—to hold it in their hands, so to speak, to examine it. When a whole school engages in textmaking, it lends itself a focus for conversations about differences and a way to resolve them—

"Well, then, let's revise the handbook," or "Let's put a different spin on the story about Mikell."

It will, of course, be obvious to readers of this book that what's good for teachers in this regard is good for children too, which is why portfolios make so much sense—they are a form of textmaking. They capture children's development, which might otherwise elude the children's notice for want of any depth of field. And just as they foster the teacher's good judgment, they also foster the children's hope.

Joseph McDonald
Brown University

APPENDIX A

The Foxfire Approach

Perspectives and Core Practices

PERSPECTIVES

This revision of what was entitled "Nine Core Practices" reflects the latest in our collective thinking about the principles and practices characteristic of the approach to instruction we pursue. The principles and practices are not scriptural; they are not oracular. They come from reflections and discussions on the results of classroom instruction. In time, we will refine them again to reflect the best of our thinking.

This approach to instruction is one of several promising approaches, some of which share many of the same principles. We've found that as each of us explores this approach in our classrooms, we broaden the base of experience from which we all work, often engaging other, resonant approaches and strategies. The approach never becomes a "recipe" for any teaching situation, nor a one-best-way teaching methodology that can be grasped through one-shot, in-service programs or teacher "handbooks."

In the contexts in which most of us work, few of us will be able to say that our instruction manifests all of these "core practices." Being able to assert that is not the point. The point is to constantly review our instructional practice. For when that happens, we and our students experience the most elegant and powerful results this approach can deliver.

The goal of schooling—and of this approach to instruction—is a more effective and humane democratic society. Individual development through schooling is a means to that goal. Often given rhetorical approval while being ignored in practice, that goal should infuse every teaching strategy and classroom activity.

As students become more thoughtful participants in their own education, our goal must be to help them become increasingly able and willing to guide their own learning, fearlessly, for the rest of their lives. Through constant evaluation of experience, and examination and application of the curriculum, they approach a state of independence, of responsible behavior, and even, in the best of all worlds, of something called wisdom.

CORE PRACTICES

1) **All the work teachers and students do together must flow from student desire, student concerns.** It must be infused from the beginning with student choice, design, revision, execution, reflection and evaluation. Teachers, of course, are still-responsible for assessing and ministering to their students' developmental needs.

   Most problems that arise during classroom activities must be solved in collaboration with students. When one asks, "Here's a situation that just came up. I don't know what to do about it. What should I do?" the teacher turns that question back to the class to wrestle with and solve, rather than simply answering it. Students are trusted continually, and all are led to the point where they embrace responsibility.

2) **Therefore, the role of the teacher must be that of collaborator and team leader and guide rather than boss.** The teacher monitors the academic and social growth of every student, leading each into new areas of understanding a competence.

   And the teacher's attitude toward students, toward the work of the class, and toward the content area being taught must model the attitudes expected of students—attitudes and values required to function thoughtfully and responsibly in a democratic society.

3) **The academic integrity of the work must be absolutely clear.** Each teacher should embrace state- or local-mandated skill content lists as "givens" to be engaged by the class, accomplish them to the level of mastery in the course of executing the class's plan, but go far beyond their normally narrow confines to discover the value and potential inherent in the content area being taught and its connections to other disciplines.

4) **The work is characterized by student action, rather than passive receipt of processed information.** Rather than students doing what they already know how to do, all must be led continually into new work and unfamiliar territory. Once skilis are "won," they must be reapplied to new problems in new ways.

   Because in such classrooms students are always operating at the very edge of their competence, it must also be made clear to them that the consequences of mistakes is not failure, but positive, constructive scrutiny of those mistakes by the rest of the class in an atmosphere where students will never be embarrassed.

5) **A constant feature of the process is its emphasis on peer teaching, small group work and teamwork.** Every student in the room is not only included, but needed, and in the end, each student can identify his or her specific stamp upon the effort. In a classroom this structured, discipline tends to take care of itself and ceases to be an issue.

6) **Connections between the classroom work and surrounding communities and the real world outside the classrooms are clear.** The content of all courses is connected to the world in which the students live. For many students, the process will engage them for the first time in identifying and characterizing the communities in which they reside.

Whenever students research larger issues like changing climate patterns, or acid rain, or prejudice, or AIDS, they must "bring them home," identifying attitudes about and illustrations and implications of those issues in their own environments.

7) **There must be an audience beyond the teacher for student work.** It may be another individual, or a small group, or the community, but it must be an audience the students want to serve, or engage, or impress. The audience, in turn, must affirm that the work is important and is needed and is worth doing—and it should, indeed, *be* all of those.

8) **As the year progresses, new activities should spiral gracefully out of the old,** incorporating lessons learned from past experiences, building on skills and understandings that can now be amplified. Rather than a finished product being regarded as the conclusion of a series of activities, it should be regarded as the starting point for a new series.

The questions that should characterize each moment of closure or completion should be, "Now what? What do we know now, and know how to do now, that we didn't know when we started out together? How can we use those skills and that information in some new, more complex and interesting ways? What's next?"

9) **As teachers, we must acknowledge the worth of aesthetic experience,** model that attitude in our interactions with students, and resist the momentum of policies and practices that deprive students of the chance to use their imaginations. We should help students produce work that is aesthetically satisfying, and help them derive the principles we employ to create beautiful work.

Because they provide the greatest sense of completeness, of the whole, of richness—the most powerful experiences are aesthetic. From those experiences we develop our capacities to appreciate, to refine, to express, to enjoy, to break out of restrictive, unproductive modes of thought.

Scientific and artistic systems embody the same principles of the relationship of life to its surroundings, and both satisfy the same fundamental needs.— John Dewey

10) **Reflection—some conscious, thoughtful time to stand apart from the work itself—is an essential activity that must take place at key points throughout the work.** It is the activity that evokes insights and nurtures revisions in our plans. It is also the activity we are least accustomed to doing, and therefore the activity we will have to be the most rigorous in including, and for which we will have to help students develop skills.

11) **The work must include unstintingly honest, ongoing evaluation for skills and content, and changes in student attitude.** A variety of strategies should be employed, combination with pre- and post-testing, ranging from simple tests of recall of simple facts through much more complex instruments involving student participation in the creation of demonstrations that answer the teacher challenge, "In what ways will you prove to me at the end of this program that you have mastered the objectives it has been designed to serve?"

Students should be trained to monitor their own progress and devise their own remediation plans, and they should be brought to the point where they can understand that the progress of each student is the concern of every student in the room.

APPENDIX B

Coalition of Essential Schools

The Common Principles

1. The school should focus on helping adolescents **learn to use their minds well.** Schools should not attempt to be "comprehensive" if such a claim is made at the expense of the school's central intellectual purpose.

2. The school's goals should be simple: that each student **master a limited number of essential skills and areas of knowledge.** While these skills and areas will, to varying degrees, reflect the traditional academic disciplines, the program's design should be shaped by the intellectual and imaginative powers and competencies that students need, rather than necessarily by "subjects" as conventionally defined. The aphorism "Less is More" should dominate: curricular decisions should be guided by the aim of thorough student mastery and achievement rather than by an effort merely to cover content.

3. The school's **goals should apply** to all students, while the means of these goals will vary as those students themselves vary. School practice should be tailor-made to meet the needs of every group or class of adolescents.

4. **Teaching and learning should be personalized** to the maximum feasible extent. Efforts should be directed toward a goal that no teacher have direct responsibility for more than 80 students. To capitalize on this personalization, decisions about the details of the course of study, the use of students' and teachers' time and the choice of teaching materials and specific pedagogies must be unreservedly placed in the hands of the principal and staff.

5. **The governing practical metaphor of the school should be student-as-worker** rather than the more familiar metaphor of teacher-as-deliverer-of-instructional-services. Accordingly, a prominent pedagogy will be coaching, to provoke students to learn how to learn and thus to teach themselves.

6. Students entering secondary school studies are those who can show competence in language and elementary mathematics. Students of tra-

ditional high school age but not yet at appropriate levels of competence to enter secondary school studies will be provided intensive remedial work to assist them quickly to meet those standards. **The diploma should be awarded upon a successful final demonstration of mastery** for graduation—an "Exhibition." This Exhibition by the student of his or her grasp of the central skills and knowledge of the school's program may be jointly administered by the faculty and by higher authorities. As the diploma is awarded when earned, the school's program proceeds with no strict age grading and with no system of "credits earned" by "time spent" in class. The emphasis is on the students' demonstration that they can do important things.

7. **The tone of the school** should explicitly and self-consciously stress values of **unanxious expectation** ("I won't threaten you but I expect much of you"), of trust (until abused) and of **decency** (the values of fairness, generosity and tolerance). Incentives appropriate to the school's particular students and teachers should be emphasized, and parents should be treated as essential collaborators.

8. **The principal and teachers should perceive themselves as generalists first** (teachers and scholars in general education) and specialists second (experts in but one particular discipline). Staff should expect multiple obligations (teacher-counselor-manager) and a sense of commitment to the entire school.

9. Ultimate administrative and budget targets should include, in addition to **total student loads per teacher of eighty or fewer pupils, substantial time for collective planning by teachers, competitive salaries for staff and an ultimate per pupil** cost not to exceed that at traditional schools by more than 10 percent. To accomplish this, administrative plans may have to show the phased reduction or elimination of some services now provided students in many traditional comprehensive secondary schools.

Any list of such brevity and specificity begs for elaboration, and it is this elaboration that must first engage the energies of each Essential school. The process of designing programs and putting them into place will take several years, and the inevitable adjustments then required will consume some years after that. Due to its complexity, school redesign is a slow and often costly business. And due to the need to adapt each design to its own constituency of students, teachers, parents, and neighborhoods and to create a strong sense of ownership of it by those who are involved, this redesign must be largely done at the level of the individual school—even as that school adheres to the principles and standards common among the Coalition member schools.

Notes

CHAPTER I

1. Teachers—but not scholars—are often referred to by first names in academic journals, emphasizing the tradition that knowledge about teaching and learning is created by those outside the classroom rather than inside. Although I want to change that tradition, I have used first names for two reasons. Cathy Skowron preferred it. In her classroom and community she is "Cathy," and would have it no other way. First names are also an indication of the peer relationship I have with the teachers that is so essential for this work. I have been a teacher for over 25 years, most recently in middle school. We did this work together.

2. Cathy's classroom might seem familiar to many of the early progressive educators; Lucy Sprague Mitchell and Carolyn Pratt would find this classroom similar to their own. For further reading, see the bibliography in Stone, 1991. More recently, whole-language classrooms have some of the same attributes. See Edelsky, Altwerger, & Flores, 1991.

CHAPTER 2

1. For an extensive discussion of teachers' oral communities, see Cochran-Smith & Lytle, 1993.

2. The Four Seasons Teleconferencing Network is designed to link the Four Seasons National Faculty for the purpose of continuing work begun in the Summer Institutes. Barb and I have used it to communicate on-line about issues that have arisen as we construct this account of practice (Baker, Obermeyer, Jervis, & Aldine, 1994).

3. The original idea was that each fall on open school night parents and children would select several pieces from the larger portfolio to pass along to the next teacher and the rest of the portfolio would go home with the family. But because this classroom is one of two in the district that spans a three-year age range, Marla and Barb have chosen to keep all the portfolios to look at growth over time. Other teachers with a two-year span are sending all but a few pieces home.

4. A district committee of parents, teachers, and administrators generates Student Learning Objectives and revises them every seven years. The last revision

was completed just before the portfolio work began. Actually, it was an attempt to assess the new Student Learning Objectives that impelled the district to develop new strategies for measuring achievement.

5. Marla makes the point that examples of children's written plans for Choice find their way into the portfolios, but products or representations of products rarely do, since Choice time is about process. However, Barb notes that "since I got a large dose of the Seven Intelligences at the Four Seasons Summer Institute, I have new eyes, so we take more photos to capture children's process, especially when what they are doing does not exist on paper. Of course, that leads to more pictures of products."

6. I am indebted to Elaine Avidon at the Institute for Literacy Studies at Lehman College for a discussion of portfolios as visible conformity.

7. This handbook, prepared by Marla for use in her school role as Portfolio Leader, is excerpted from a larger district handbook, which is not for circulation or quotation lest teachers miss the opportunity to develop their own portfolios in their own contexts.

8. The pass-along portfolios are compiled differently by each teacher. Marla and Barb have kept their entire portfolios in the classroom to look at the three-year span of work. Marla has instituted a ritual when children move to fourth grade. In the fall of fourth grade, the child makes an appointment with the fourth-grade teacher. When the appointment is confirmed, the child takes the portfolio from Marla; the new teacher and the child together pick what will go in the pass-along portfolio. The rest of the portfolio goes home. In telling this Marla recounts how a fourth-grade teacher used to think that the portfolios were too narrow, but in preparing the pass-along portfolio with her former students, he has begun to see the power portfolios have for children.

CHAPTER 3

1. For another case where early childhood norms matter, see Meier, 1991.

2. At the time of the study, there were three African-American women, but Tamara Harper died of cancer during the year.

3. Another Coalition school, Central Park East Secondary School (CPESS), has attracted national attention from educators and the media for its success with urban students who fall below the poverty line. CPESS does not enroll nearly the wide range of students that Fenway does, nor does CPESS encounter the problems with transiency that Fenway faces. See Bensman, 1995.

4. Lawrence R. Velvel is dean of the Massachusetts School of Law and editor-in-Chief of the law journal *The Long Term View*. He says: "When the history of the last 30 years or so of academia is written at a decent remove in the future, such as 50 years from today, historians will look back in horror at academia's conduct with regard to the tests. Historians will consider the academic world to have acted reprehensibly" (1993, p. 3). He identifies three aspects that crystallize his argument: (1) It is easier to judge candidates by number and no matter how many time testers

say that tests should not be the only measure, the cautionary guidelines are un-heeded; (2) though real life calls for the careful, deliberative, methodical ways, the tests reward "speededness"; and (3) the tests have caused emotional blight—the ruination of lives because no matter how wrongly, tests have been taken as shatter-ing proof of inferiority.

Bibliography

Anderson, Beverly. (1993). The stages of systemic change. *Educational leadership, 51*(1), 14–17.

Armstrong, Thomas. (1993, September 1). Home is where the learning is: 25 ways to help your child. *Family Circle*, 84.

Baker, Terry; Obermeyer, Gary; Jervis, Kathe; & Aldine, Susan. (1994). *Saving face to face: Network moderators and the construction of collaborative space for school restructuring.* Paper presented at the American Educational Research Association, New Orleans, LA.

Bellevue (WA) Public Schools. (1993). *Bellevue literacy composite portfolio: Staff handbook, 1992–1993.* Bellevue, WA: Author.

Bensman, David. (1995). *Learning to think well: Central Park East Secondary School graduates reflect on their experiences in high school and college.* New York: National Center for Restructuring Education, Schools, and Teaching (NCREST).

Carini, Patricia. (1991). *Images and immeasurables.* Presentation to the North Dakota Study Group on Evaluation, Woodstock, IL.

Chittenden, Edward. (1991). Authentic assessment, evaluation, and documentation. In Vito Perrone (Ed.), *Expanding assessment* (pp. 22–31). Washington, DC: Association for Supervision and Curriculum Development.

Cochran-Smith, Marilyn, & Lytle, Susan L. (1993). *Inside/outside: Teacher research and knowledge.* New York: Teachers College Press.

Darling-Hammond, Linda. (1993). Reframing the school reform agenda: Developing capacity for school transformation. *Phi Delta Kappan, 74*(10), 753–761.

Delpit, Lisa. (1993). The silenced dialogue: Power of pedagogy in educating other people's children. In Lois Weis & Michelle Fine (Eds.), *Beyond silenced voices: Class, race, and gender in United States schools* (pp. 119–139). Albany: State University of New York Press.

Dewey, John. (1916). *Democracy and education.* New York: Macmillan.

Edelsky, Carole; Altwerger, Bess; & Flores, Barbara. (1991). *Whole language: What's the difference?* Portsmouth, NH: Heinemann.

Equity in educational assessment. (1994). [Special issue] (Sean Reardon, Kate Scott, & John Verre, eds.). *Harvard Educational Review, 64*(1).

English, Marla Rae, & Renfrow-Baker, Barbara. (1993). *Class handbook 1-2-3.* Bellevue, WA: Bellevue Public Schools.

Fenway Middle College High School. (1991–1992). *Speak for yourself.* Boston, MA: Author.

Fox, Mem. (1993). *Radical reflections–passionate opinions about teaching, learning, and living.* San Diego: Harcourt Brace.

Gardner, Howard. (1991). *The unschooled mind: How children think and how schools should teach.* New York: Basic Books.

Geertz, Clifford. (1973). *The interpretation of cultures.* New York: Basic Books.

Greene, Maxine. (1993). Diversity and inclusion: Toward a curriculum for human beings. *Teachers College Record, 95*(2), 211–221.

Hawkins, David. (1970). I, thou, it. In *The ESS reader* (pp. 45–52). Newton, MA: The Education Development Center.

Jervis, Kathe. (1986). A teacher's quest for a child's questions. *Harvard Educational Review, 56*(2), 132–150.

Kalan, Robert, & Crews, Donald. (1991). *Rain.* New York: Mulberry Books.

Koepke, Mary. (1992, March). All in the family. *Teacher Magazine* , pp. 21–23.

Martin-Kniep, Giselle. (1993). Authentic assessment in practice. *Holistic Education Review, 6*(1), 52–58.

McDonald, Joseph. (1992). Three pictures at an exhibition. *Studies on Exhibitions* (No.1). Providence, RI: Coalition of Essential Schools.

Meier, Deborah. (1991). The kindergarten tradition in the high school. In Kathe Jervis & Carol Montag (Eds.), *Progressive education in the 1990s: Transforming practice* (pp. 135–148). New York: Teachers College Press.

Nicholls, John, & Hazzard, Susan. (1993). *Education as adventure.* New York: Teachers College Press.

Patterns in Mathematics: Student Materials. (1993). *A unit of core high school mathematics from the interactive mathematics program.* Emeryville, CA.

Perrone, Vito. (1991). Large purposes. In Kathe Jervis & Carol Montag (Eds.), *Progressive education in the 1990s: Transforming practice* (pp. 9–16). New York: Teachers College Press.

Prospect Archive and Center for Educational and Research. (1986). *The Prospect Center documentary processes: In progress.* North Bennington, VT: Author.

Provincetown Public Schools Faculty. (1991). *Portfolio assessment using a multidimensional approach to evaluating student learning.* Provincetown, MA: Author.

Seidel, Steve, & Walters, Joseph. (1994, December). The "things" children make in school: Disposable or indispensable? *Harvard Graduate School Alumni Bulletin,* pp. 18–20.

Sizer, Theodore. (1984). *Horace's compromise: The dilemma of the American high school.* Boston: Houghton Mifflin.

Skowron, Cathy. (1992). Essential aspects of visual arts learning: A personal point of view. Unpublished master's thesis, Goddard College, Plainfield, VT.

Southworth, Robert. (1992). *Habits of mind.* Paper presented at the New England Educational Research Organization Annual Conference, Portsmouth, NH.

Stone, Marie Kirchner. (1991). Progressive education bibliography (1880–1990). In Kathe Jervis & Carol Montag (Eds.), *Progressive education in the 1990s: Transforming practice* (pp. 189–196). New York: Teachers College Press.

Travers, P. L. (1969). Only connect. In Sheila Egoff, G. T. Stubbs, & L. F. Ashley (Eds.), *Only connect: Readings on children's literature* (pp. 183–206). Toronto: Oxford University Press.

Valencia, Sheila, & Place, Nancy. (1993). Literacy portfolios for teaching, learning, and accountability: The Bellevue Literacy Assessment Project." In Elfrieda Hiebert, Sheila Valencia, & Peter Afflerbach (Eds.), *Authentic literacy assessment: Practices and possibilities* (pp. 134–156). Newark, DE: International Reading Association.

Velvel, Lawrence R. (1993). Are standardized tests contributing to social stratification? *The Long Term View* [Massachusetts School of Law at Andover], *1*(4), 3–4.

Wolf, Dennie Palmer. (1994). Curriculum and assessment standards: Common measures or conversations?" In Nina Cobb (Ed.), *The future of education: Perspectives on national standards in America* (pp. 85–106). New York: College Entrance Examination Board.

Index

About the Author

Kathe Jervis is Senior Research Associate at the National Center for Restructuring Education, Schools, and Teaching (NCREST) at Teachers College, Columbia University. For over 25 years, she has taught K-12 and college students in Massachusetts, California, and New York, most recently as a NYC District #3 middle school science teacher and as an adjunct assistant professor in early childhood at City College, CUNY. A founding editor of *Pathways: A Forum for Progressive Educators*, she co-edited (with Carol Montag) *Progressive Education for the 1990's: Transforming Practice* (Teachers College Press, 1991). She participates in national educational communities such as the Prospect Center for Education and Research and the North Dakota Study Group on Evaluation and writes on assessment, teachers' inquiry into practice, and issues of race and ethnicity. She has an M.A. in Medieval History from New York University and an M.A. in Human Development from Pacific Oaks in Pasadena, California.